vim scan hp2

'pttwl. pkg , 93a 75. msg'

Easy Word
Processing
for the Older
Generation

Vins Scan

Wuredir . cab. bak

Other Books of Interest

*****

Easy Word Processing for the Older Generation

Jim Gatenby

BERNARD BABANI (publishing) LTD
The Grampians
Shepherds Bush Rd
London W6 7NF
England

www.babanibooks.com

Please Note

Although every care has been taken with the production of this book to ensure that any projects, designs, modifications and/or programs, etc., contained herewith, operate in a correct and safe manner and also that any components specified are normally available in Great Britain, the Publishers and Author do not accept responsibility in any way for the failure (including fault in design) of any project, design, modification or program to work correctly or to cause damage to any equipment that it may be connected to or used in conjunction with, or in respect of any other damage or injury that may be so caused, nor do the Publishers accept responsibility in any way for the failure to obtain specified components.

Notice is also given that if equipment that is still under warranty is modified in any way or used or connected with home-built equipment then that warranty may be void.

© 2005 BERNARD BABANI (publishing) LTD

First published - September 2005
Reprinted - December 2005
Reprinted - February 2006

British Library Cataloguing in Publication Data:

A catalogue record for this book is available from the
British Library

ISBN 0 85934 609 9
Cover Design by Gregor Arthur
Printed and bound in Great Britain by Cox and Wyman Ltd

About this Book

Microsoft Word, on which this book is based, is arguably one of the most creative and useful pieces of computer software ever created; it's very easy to use yet extremely powerful and versatile. You don't need special skills or technical knowledge to obtain results of a professional standard. Word can be used, for example, to help you communicate with friends and family with greetings and invitations or to apply for a job, run a small business, advertise events or publish your memoirs. Perhaps, like me, you could use Word to provide an income in retirement while working in the comfort of your own home. This book is part of the very successful "Older Generation" series from Bernard Babani (publishing) Ltd which includes my best-selling book "Computing for the Older Generation".

Early chapters of this new book outline the scope of the modern word processor, the equipment needed and basic skills such as the use of the keyboard. A rudimentary knowledge of the Windows operating system, which controls all aspects of computer activity, is essential and is covered in a separate chapter. Help is also given for those with special needs, such as impaired vision or mobility.

Microsoft Word and the Microsoft Works word processor are discussed before getting down to the basics of entering text, saving on disc and editing, formatting and printing. Tasks such as typing a letter and saving your own letterhead are also described.

Pictures from a digital camera, etc., can be inserted into Word to enliven a document or personalize a family letter, for example. These topics are described in some detail, including the moving, resizing and cropping of pictures after insertion into a Word document. Text in a newspaper-style format of two or more columns is also discussed.

Smaller documents such as flyers, invitations, greetings cards, etc., may require a more light-hearted approach. The Word program offers a huge range of different fonts or styles of lettering and these can be manipulated in different shapes, using the WordArt feature. Ready-made templates contain all the design and artwork for a stunning creation such as a greeting card, invitation, advert or business card. These more exotic features are discussed in a separate chapter "Getting Creative".

Many people in retirement have the time to satisfy a long-held ambition to produce a booklet, magazine or complete book; this might be a history of their town or village, their former company or their hobby. Alternatively it could be a novel or a definitive work on a subject for which they have vast experience. The production of such longer documents including page numbering, headers and footers and various page layouts is covered in a separate chapter. The insertion into a Word document of extracts from other programs, such as a spreadsheet, is also explained.

The final chapter shows how Word files and folders can be organized into an efficient hierarchy or tree structure and how to delete, copy or move files and folders between different locations. Larger word processing projects require a reliable system of backups, i.e. duplicate copies of important work. This is covered together with essential precautions to keep your computer free from viruses and attack from Internet "hackers". Sending Word files as e-mail attachments is described in detail.

The Appendices cover the Mail Merge Wizard used for producing personalized versions of a letter and the Office Clipboard, for copying, cutting and pasting multiple items.

My aim has been to produce a book which is useful and easy to read and to pass on helpful word processing and computing experience gained over more than 20 years.

About the Author

Jim Gatenby trained as a Chartered Mechanical Engineer and initially worked at Rolls-Royce Ltd using computers in the analysis of jet engine performance. He obtained a Master of Philosophy degree in Mathematical Education by research at Loughborough University of Technology and taught mathematics and computing to 'A' Level for many years. His most recent posts included Head of Computer Studies and Information Technology Coordinator. During this time he has written many books in the fields of educational computing and Microsoft Windows.

The author, himself a member of the over 60s club, has considerable experience of teaching students in school and adult education on GCSE Computing and Computer Literacy and Information Technology (CLAIT) courses.

Trademarks

Microsoft, MSN, Microsoft Word, Works Windows, Windows Explorer, Windows Update and Windows XP are either trademarks or registered trademarks of Microsoft Corporation. F-Secure, Virus Protection and Internet Shield are either trademarks or registered trademarks of F-Secure Corporation. Norton AntiVirus is a trademark of Symantec Corporation. McAfee VirusScan is a registered trademark of McAfee, Inc. Adobe Acrobat is a trademark of Adobe Systems Incorporated. Google is a trademark of Google, Inc.

All other brand and product names used in this book are recognized as trademarks or registered trademarks, of their respective companies.

Contents

1

2

3

4

5

6

Editing and Formatting 109

7

Introducing Desktop Publishing 123

Introduction

What is Word Processing?

Nowadays the term word processor refers to a *program* which you can buy on a CD and install on your computer, along with all of your other software, such as programs to surf the Internet or send e-mails, for example. Modern word processing programs are much more than a replacement for the typewriter. They are extremely versatile and capable of producing all sorts of documents and publications, such as the text book shown below.

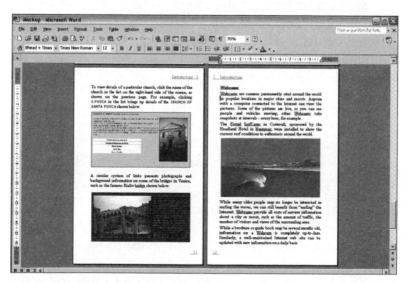

Although very powerful, modern word processors are very easy to use – you don't need to be a trained typist although it's a good idea to acquire some basic keyboard skills.

Word Processing – A Brief Overview

The following are the basic word processing operations, although they may not always be completed in the order shown. All of the tasks are discussed in detail later in this book.

Entering Text

Text is typed in using the keyboard. You may prefer to prepare a rough, hand-written draft initially. This will allow you to concentrate on the composition of the document without having to worry about the computing skills. Eventually you will probably be able to type your ideas straight into the computer when your typing skills improve.

Saving a Document

A permanent copy of a document is saved on a magnetic disc for future use. A document saved on disc is often called a *file*. A file can be retrieved from disc and displayed on the screen where it can be amended or added to.

Printing a Document

A copy of the document is printed on paper so that it can be read away from the computer or filed away for record purposes.

Editing a Document

A document can be amended on the screen to correct spelling or grammatical mistakes or to change the content. Software such as Microsoft Word and the Microsoft Works word processor have built-in spelling and grammar checkers and a thesaurus. Editing can take place while the text is initially being entered; alternatively you can edit an existing document after it has been retrieved from a disc.

Formatting a Document

This involves the many special effects which alter the appearance of a document. These include the layout of the page, the size of the margins, the line spacing and text effects such as:

- **Bold**
- *Italics*
- Underlined.

Other formatting features include the automatic numbering of lists; a list may also be highlighted using *bullets*, in various shapes and sizes, as shown in the small list above.

Formatting effects can be switched on before a document is initially entered; alternatively effects can be applied to an existing document which has been retrieved from a disc and displayed on the screen.

Desktop Publishing Effects

As discussed later, modern word processing programs include many *desktop publishing* features such as different *fonts* (styles and sizes of lettering) and text in newspaper style columns.

Pictures can also be included within a page of text and there are different ways of flowing the text around the picture. The picture can be moved around the page and enlarged or made smaller to achieve the desired result.

The WordArt feature allows text to be manipulated into various shapes as shown below.

Word Processing Software

The material in this book is based on two closely-related word processors. The first is Microsoft Word, the most popular word processing program in the world, used in most business and office computers. The second is the word processor supplied as part of the Microsoft Works package installed on many new home computers. The two programs are shown on the right listed in

an extract from the **Start** menu in the Microsoft Windows system used to operate most computers.

Both of these word processing programs are easy to use, yet capable of carrying out the most demanding of tasks.

Even in this electronic age the production of documents on paper is still important for all types of communication. You can even use a program like Microsoft Word to produce Web pages for display on the Internet. Not surprisingly word processing is probably the most common use of computers in the world today.

In fact, the modern word processing system is light years ahead of its early ancestor, the typewriter, and has three major advantages:

- The word processor is much easier to use
- It is far more versatile
- It is much more efficient.

These assertions are discussed on the following pages.

Word Processors are Easy to Use

Anyone can produce stylish documents without any particular skill or training. However, it may help to look at a few professional documents first, to get some ideas about style and layout. Many of us tend to overdo the fancy text effects when first let loose on a word processor.

Icons

One of the reasons why the word processor is easy to use is because many of the main tasks are represented on the screen as *icons* or small pictures, as shown below. All you have to do is move a mouse pointer over the required screen object then "click" or press a button on the mouse.

For example, the three icons shown below on the right are used, reading from left to right, to print a document, launch the spelling and grammar checker and cut or remove a piece of text.

It is no longer necessary to learn complex commands in what seemed like a foreign language. Nowadays all you need to do is familiarize yourself with the icons for the various tasks. If you let the mouse pointer hover over an icon, a message pops up giving the icon's function, such as starting a **New Blank Document**, as shown on the right.

Menus

As an alternative to using icons, some tasks are listed in *menus* which drop down on the screen. Shown below is an extract from the **File** menu in Microsoft Word. When you click over the word **File** on the left of the Menu Bar across the top of the screen, the **File** menu drops down as shown in the extract below. Similar drop-down menus appear under **Edit, View**, and **Insert**, etc.

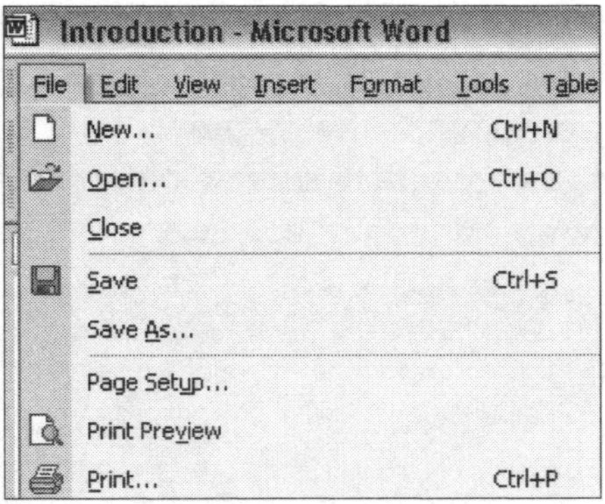

As shown above, the **File** menu includes some of the most common word processing operations, such as starting a new document, opening an existing one (retrieving from disc), saving on disc and printing on paper. To launch a particular operation from the menu, such as **Save**, for example, it is only necessary to click the word in the list of menu options, as shown above.

Keyboard Shortcuts

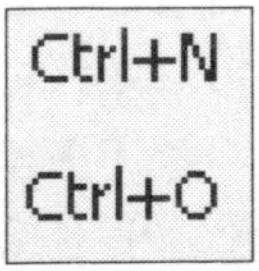

Please note that the letters at the right-hand side of the above menu are key presses which can be used as an alternative to clicking with the mouse. **Ctrl** is short for the **Control** key. These topics are discussed in more detail later in this book.

Ctrl+N

Ctrl+O

Word Processors are Versatile

To illustrate the range of activities possible with a modern word processing program, here are a few sample tasks which anyone can easily accomplish without any special skill or training.

Letters to Friends and Family, etc.

You can easily produce letters and longer documents, for example, to keep in touch with your friends and family. These might include family photographs incorporated within the text. Documents produced in a word processor can be attached to e-mails and sent (immediately) anywhere in the world, avoiding the cost, delay and inconvenience of conventional postage.

Swallows Barn
Millers Dale
Staffordshire
SA3 ML6
5 June 2005

The Manager
The Eden Hotel
Chianciano Terme
Tuscany

Dear Sir/Madam

A friend has recommended your hotel to me and I would like to arrange a holiday with you in May 2006, if possible.

I would be most grateful if you could send me a copy of your latest brochure, including details of your facilities for the disabled and car hire.

I understand that your town is famous for its health-giving mineral springs; I would therefore be grateful for any further information you can provide on the various spas.

Yours faithfully

John Williamson

Posters, Invitations, Cards and Flyers, etc.

You can create attractive posters to promote a local event such as a charity evening or a sponsored walk. This could include various *desktop publishing* effects, such as different styles and sizes of text and drawings and pictures, known as *clip-art*. Using similar word processing techniques you can:

- Design a business card or a flyer to promote a small business you might be starting up.
- Prepare your own greeting cards and invitations.

Documents created in Microsoft Word and Works can be based on ready-made *templates* such as the birthday card shown below.

All you have to do is to select the required template then enter your own text to replace the "dummy" words initially provided in the template.

Longer Documents

The word processing program enables you to produce professional-looking reports and documents. You might, for example, produce a report about a local issue such as a planning or a road safety matter, for example. This could include bulleted lists, graphs, photographs and tables of figures. Or you might want to write about your favourite holiday destination, including photographs you have taken.

Venice

ST.MARK'S SQUARE

There is so much to see in Venice that you may need more than one visit to take in the major sights. A good place to start is St. Mark's Square. The square was originally just a space in front of the Basilica of St. Mark, the private chapel of the Doge or head of the Venetian state.

As well as the magnificent architecture of the Basilica, there are shops and open air cafés around the square. The Basilica was originally dedicated to St. Mark in 832 but was destroyed by fire in an uprising in 976. The ruined buildings were restored and consecrated in 1094. Next to St. Mark's Basilica is the Ducal or Doge's Palace, started in the 9th century and built for the Doge and the justices of Venice.

THE BRIDGE OF SIGHS

This connects the Doge's palace to the Prisons and derives its name from the reaction of the prisoners on their way to begin their sentences.

THE GRAND CANAL

Perhaps the greatest wonder of Venice is its location in the lagoon off the mainland of Italy. The Grand Canal through the middle of Venice and the network of smaller canals around it are the main route by which most visitors arrive and all supplies are delivered to the city. As there are no cars or lorries this makes walking around the city a great pleasure.

Of course, no visit to Venice would be complete without a ride on the canals in one of the many famous Gondolas.

Magazines, Newsletters and Books

Many people use word processors to publish a regular magazine or newsletter for a club, church or community, with text in two or more columns in a similar format to a newspaper. Alternatively you could write your life story for your family archives or document the history of your town or village.

Some older people have an urge to publish their own text book or write their first novel; as a senior citizen myself, the word processor has enabled me to become a self-employed author of over 20 books such as this one. Everything in the finished book, including the final layout and graphics, has been produced using the word processing program Microsoft Word. An extract from an earlier book created in Microsoft Word is shown below.

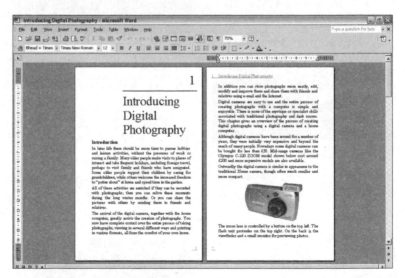

The word processor displays the pages on the screen just as they will appear in the finished book.

Word Processors are Efficient

Some of the advantages of the word processor, compared with traditional methods such as the manual typewriter are:

- Corrections can be made on the screen before printing on paper, so there is no evidence of any alterations. Several copies can easily be printed.

- Documents are saved on disc, then retrieved later. This allows a document to be used again, perhaps with small changes such as a new date. There is no need to spend time retyping the whole document.

- Text can be *edited* more easily – whole blocks of text can be inserted, deleted or moved to a new position in the document.

- The *Find and Replace* feature enables a word (or group of words) to be exchanged for another word or words, wherever they occur in a document. For example, replace "house" with "property".

- Text can be formatted with effects such as bold and italic and in various fonts (styles of lettering) as shown in the French Script example below.

French Script

- The layout of the page can easily be changed, with different margins, line spacing, pictures, photographs and newspaper-style columns.

- Very little force is needed to operate a computer keyboard compared with the manual typewriter.

Modern word processors contain many additional features such as spelling and grammar checkers, a thesaurus and a word count facility.

Glossary of Word Processing Terms

Backup

Duplicate or backup copies of important work are often made for security, on a CD or a removable hard disc drive.

Clip-Art

Libraries of ready-made pictures, drawings, cartoons and photographs which can be included in a document.

Desktop Publishing Effects

These include a wide choice of *fonts* or styles and sizes of lettering, text manipulated into different shapes and text in columns. Also pictures/photos incorporated into the page.

Editing a Document

Editing involves correcting spelling or grammatical mistakes or changing the content or layout. Modern word processors usually include built-in spelling and grammar checkers and a thesaurus.

File

This is any sort of document or program saved on a magnetic disc. In word processing a file might be anything from a small business card, invitation or greeting card or letters, reports to a complete book or magazine.

Formatting a Document

This involves changing the appearance of a document by setting the page layout, sizes of margins, line spacing and effects such as italics, underlined text, tables and bullets.

Icon

An icon is a small picture on the screen representing an operation such as printing, saving on disc, etc. Operations are launched by "clicking" the appropriate icon.

Keyboard Shortcuts

Combinations of key presses used to perform various operations as an alternative to using the mouse. For example, **Ctrl+P** causes the current document to be printed. (**Ctrl+P** means hold down the key marked **Ctrl** and simultaneously press the **P** key.)

Magnetic Disc

Originally documents were saved on small removable magnetic or "floppy" discs, now largely replaced by removable CDs and hard discs inside of the computer.

Menu

A list of operations or options which drops down on the screen when selected from the Menu Bar. Operations are initiated by "clicking" the appropriate option in the menu.

Microsoft Office

A suite of programs which includes Microsoft Word and several other important programs. The current version at the time of writing is called Microsoft Office XP.

Microsoft Windows

This is the program used to "drive" or operate most computers and is known as the *operating system*. It works in the background whenever you are using the computer and is used for controlling the screen display, the menus, and all of the *peripheral devices* such as disc drives, printers, keyboard, etc. The current version at the time of writing is called Microsoft Windows XP.

Microsoft Word

This is the leading word processing program used in business and by professional and home users worldwide.

Microsoft Works

A suite of several programs designed to do a range of tasks including word processing, spreadsheet (accounts, etc.), database (for keeping records) and a calendar, amongst other things. Microsoft Works includes a similar word processor to Microsoft Word.

Mouse

A small hand-held device used to move a pointer around the screen to point at and select, by "clicking", icons and menu options.

Printing a Document

Making a copy of a document on paper so that it can be perused away from the computer.

Program

A set of instructions stored inside the computer. Separate programs are used for tasks such as word processing, drawing, accounts, or surfing the Internet, etc. A new program is usually purchased on one or more CDs and copied onto the computer's internal hard disc. The program can then be "run" from the hard disc whenever it is needed. The original CD(s) should be stored away in a safe place.

Saving a Document

Making a permanent copy of a document, usually on the *hard disc* built into the computer.

Template

A ready-made design for a document such as a poster which you can tailor to your own requirements. Your own words can be added to replace the "dummy" text provided.

Creating a Home Office

This section looks at the preparations needed to create the right environment for word processing in your home. The place where you work at the computer will be referred to as the "home office" although in practice this may be no more than a corner of your living room or bedroom, etc. It may be worth considering the following points:

- Where is the best location for the computer?
- What additional furniture is needed?
- What computing equipment is needed?

Choosing a Location for Your Home Office

Obvious constraints on the siting of your computer are the available free space in your home, the amount of money you have to spend and the sort of "work" you intend to do with the computer. In my experience, if you are able to create a professional-standard working environment, this will be reflected in the quality of the material you are able to produce.

If you are intending to do demanding work with the word processor – for example, starting a small business, producing a magazine or writing a novel – then ideally you need a separate area where you can work away from household distractions. You also need plenty of desk space for laying out documents; some shelves and at least one filing cabinet can be very useful.

Initially I worked in a small office built into the corner of our garage; although quite Spartan, this had the advantage of being separate from the house, so that it felt almost like going out to work.

When our sons left home I was able to move into a spare bedroom and enjoy the luxury of carpets and central heating.

Another popular solution for a home office is to use a shed or summerhouse in the garden, although this can be expensive to set up initially.

Your home office should, if possible, be located in a secure place in your home or garden – computing equipment is a favourite target for burglars. It's also a good idea to mark expensive items, perhaps with your postcode, for example. This can be done invisibly with an infra-red security pen Visible marking with a permanent marker may act as a deterrent to thieves.

Power Points

Several power points are necessary for a complete word processing system including printer and scanner, etc. Trailing extension leads are untidy and potentially dangerous and power points built into a wall are preferable.

Telephone Sockets

Most people these days want an Internet connection, so you need at least one telephone socket near to the computer. If you can afford to subscribe to a *broadband* Internet service, this will allow you to have an ordinary telephone on your desk and use it at the same time as the Internet.

You can provide an extra telephone socket using one of the cheap extension leads available from most DIY stores. This may involve drilling holes in walls, etc., and perhaps threading the cable through the roof space of your home.

Networking Two or More Computers

If you have more than one computer in your home, you may wish to consider setting up a network. This will allow several computers to share one Internet connection. You can also transfer files, i.e. documents, etc., between networked computers Traditional networks use cables to connect computers but this often involves drilling walls and trailing cables around the house or office. A *wireless network* allows computers around the house to share resources such as files, printers and an Internet connection without the need for trailing cables or holes drilled in walls.

With a wireless network, one computer is connected to a convenient telephone socket but any further computers can be located anywhere in the house (or garden). These additional computers are connected to the first computer by radio frequency signals.

After several years of using a network based on cables I have recently changed to a wireless network. This was surprisingly easy to set up – it really was a genuine case of "plug and play".

Our home network now consists of a desktop computer for general family use and a second desktop machine used solely for word processing or "typesetting" computer books. We also have a laptop machine which can be used anywhere in the house or garden. The wireless network means you can use a laptop computer to work (or play) in the garden on a summer's day and still be connected to the Internet. A wireless network is also ideal if your home office is based in a garden shed or summerhouse, as there is no need to install any network cables across the garden.

Furniture for Your Home Office

If you intend to spend long hours word processing, then a number of health factors need to be considered. Correct posture is essential, so if possible buy an adjustable office chair and a special computer desk or work station. Repetitive Strain Injury (RSI) is a well-known consequence of long hours spent typing, so it is essential to adjust your seat height to give a comfortable working position, with arms roughly level. Frequent stretching exercises and regular breaks away from the keyboard – every hour, say – are often recommended to avoid this problem.

Over the years I have obtained some good furniture bargains from firms specializing in second-hand office desks, chairs and cabinets, etc. Quite often this includes purpose-built computer desks which are as good as new. Second-hand office furniture from the business world tends to be more robust and of higher quality than the "flat packs" sold in some of the large stores.

Self-Employment Issues

A word processor can be used to earn extra income in retirement. You might, for example, take on work for local businesses and organizations such as colleges and universities. A modern word processor such as Microsoft Word, etc., can certainly be used for all sorts of commercial activities such as producing advertising posters, leaflets, business cards or invitations and typesetting books such as this one.

During your working life you are likely to have acquired valuable skills which might lead to consultancy work in your particular field. The results of your deliberations will need to be presented in report form to a high standard. There may be opportunities for some part-time teaching in your area, in a subject in which you have experience. Or you might be able to teach basic skills such as adult literacy and numeracy. Teaching notes and handouts for students need to be well presented these days – handwritten notes and documents containing obvious typing corrections are no longer acceptable. You need to have competence with a word processor for all of these activities.

When setting up a small business many of your start-up costs can be deducted from your profits and so reduce your tax bill. Certainly any office equipment and furniture will be eligible, as well as the cost of heating and lighting the office area as a fraction of your household bills.

You should also seek professional advice to find out the tax and insurance implications of becoming self-employed and working from home. You will need to register as self-employed and, above a certain income, pay the appropriate National Insurance contributions.

A Few Myths About Computers

- **Older people can't use computers.** False. I am over sixty and my oldest ever student was in his eighties. A friend in his seventies builds and repairs computers as a small business; unfortunately he can't get on his own computer because his mother-in-law (in her 90s) is always using it! *Accessibility features* are provided in Microsoft Windows to help people with mobility or eyesight problems.

- **Computers are of no use to older people**. Older people have the time to learn new skills and to develop hobbies involving word processing. These might include producing newsletters and magazines for clubs and community groups. Letters and documents can be improved by word processing and including photographs, etc.

- **Computers are always breaking down.** I have several computers and there have been no major problems in the last five years.

- **Computers are difficult to use.** The advent of the "graphical user interface" means you don't have to learn complicated commands. You just point at icons (little pictures on the screen) and click a mouse button in order to carry out a task.

- **You can easily lose hours of work.** An author once lost an entire novel representing about a year's hard work. However, making *backup copies*, as discussed later in this book, should prevent you from losing important work. Using these cheap and simple methods I have managed to produce over 20 books without ever losing a single page of text.

Word Processing Equipment

Obtaining a Computer

Most people buy a type of computer known as a PC – after the original IBM Personal Computer. This standard of machine, also sometimes referred to as "IBM compatible", is dominant in home and business computing worldwide.

There are many different manufacturers of PC-type computers but they all conform to the same standard; the PC is the "platform" for which the majority of new software (i.e. programs) is developed. PCs are readily available in many large stores and mail order companies supplying new machines and components at what seem to be very low prices compared with a few years ago. At the time of writing you can buy a new computer system, often containing a printer and software (including a word processing program), for under £500. However, if you are working to a tight budget, you could probably pick up a perfectly adequate second-hand machine for under £100. Word processing is not a very demanding task for a computer and it's certainly not essential to have the very latest equipment.

It's a good idea to try to find a small local company, with a good reputation, perhaps employing only a few people. They usually build new computers, carry out repairs and if necessary visit your home to install the system and connect it to the Internet.

The Parts of a Word Processing System

The next few pages discuss briefly some of the essential components of computer systems – but only to the extent that they are relevant to word processing.

The essential components discussed here are:

- The keyboard
- The mouse
- The screen or monitor
- The tower or base unit
- The hard disc drive
- The CD/ DVD drive
- The printer
- The scanner
- The digital camera
- The Internet connection.

Shown above is a complete word processing system including computer, laser printer and a scanner on the left.

The Keyboard

Keyboards have been around since the first typewriters but they have not yet been replaced, to any great extent, by modern inventions such as voice recognition systems.

Most keyboards still follow the **QWERTY** convention, which refers to the order of the first six letter keys as shown above and below.

Keyboards and typing skills are discussed in more detail later in this book. Many people, including myself, don't learn to type properly and consequently waste a lot of time, especially in the early stages of word processing. It's worth acquiring some keyboard skills, perhaps by investing in a *typing tutor* program.

The Mouse

The mouse is a small hand-held device containing two or three buttons and is used to move a pointer around the screen. Screen objects such as icons (small pictures) and options on a menu are selected by pointing and "clicking" the left mouse button.

The mouse can typically be used for tasks such as:

- Starting programs from a screen icon
- Opening a "folder" containing documents
- Displaying a menu and selecting an option.

Shown below is an extract from the Windows **Start** menu. Any of the programs or features can be launched by clicking the left mouse button while the pointer is over the name or icon.

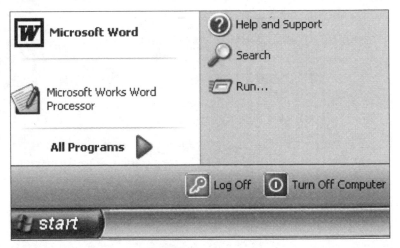

These topics are discussed in more detail later in the chapter on Microsoft Windows.

The Monitor

The choice of monitor (or screen) depends on how much you want to spend. Typical monitor sizes range from 15 inches through to 22 inches. These measurements are measured diagonally across the screen and are nominal. The actual viewing area may be about an inch less, because of the plastic case surrounding the *CRT* (Cathode Ray Tube). If you intend to do a lot of exacting work such as DeskTop Publishing or Graphics, or if you have impaired vision, try to obtain the largest screen you can afford. CRT monitors typically cost £60-£350.

Very slim, flat screens (known as *TFT* monitors) are now available; these are more expensive (typically £130 upwards) but ideal if you're limited for desk space.

Enlarging the Screen Display

The Microsoft Windows XP operating system supplied with most new PC computers includes a screen **Magnifier** to help anyone with impaired vision. This enables any section of the screen to be enlarged and viewed in its own window.

The Magnifier is one of a number of **Accessibility Features** provided in Windows XP and discussed later in this book. You can also change the *resolution*, i.e. the size of the text and screen objects such as icons, as discussed later.

Improving the Quality of the Display

Please note that the quality of the screen display depends not only on the monitor but also on the electronic components in the computer used to produce the on-screen graphics. These components are often supplied on a *graphics card*, a small circuit board plugged into the computer's main *motherboard*. Alternatively the graphics may be controlled by electronics components built into the motherboard – often referred to as "on board" graphics. It is often possible to improve the screen display (for graphics, etc.) by fitting a high performance graphics card.

The Base Unit

The *base unit* is at the heart of the computer system. Nowadays the base unit is often in the form of a *tower*, as shown on the right. This can stand upright on the floor, thereby saving desk space.

This creates a less cluttered desk, with more space for documents, as shown below.

Desktop base units are also available as flat boxes on which the monitor can be placed.

The base unit contains essential components of the computer such as the *processor*, the *memory*, the *motherboard*, the *hard disc drive*, the *CD/DVD drive* and the *floppy disc drive*. The components in the base unit are connected to the main circuit board of the computer, known as the *motherboard*.

CD/DVD Drives

Many computers are now supplied with a combined CD and DVD drive, known as a "combo" drive. These are capable of reading existing CDs and DVDs and some can also write (i.e. record) new CDs and DVDs.

A DVD drive or combined CD/DVD drive will, for example, allow you to relax by watching a film on your computer after slaving for hours over the word processor.

Floppy Disc Drive

The smallest slot on the base unit is the floppy disc drive. Floppy discs are declining in popularity since their storage capacity is very limited compared with CDs. 3½ Floppy (A:)

CD versus Floppy Disc

A CD-R costing a few pence can store several hundred times as much data as a floppy disc. I use CD-Rs for making backups (i.e. security copies) of all of my work – a floppy disc is too small to hold say, a chapter of this book, for example. A CD-R can hold several books such as this one, including screenshots and photographs, which take up a lot of storage space.

The Processor

This is the "brains" of the computer and carries out all of the instructions sent into the processor by the program you are using. Well known brands are the Intel Pentium and Celeron and the AMD Athlon. The speed at which the processor works determines the performance of the computer. Currently new computers are being advertised offering processor speeds of around 3GHz. This is a measure of how many thousands of millions of instructions per second the processor can carry out.

Machines with faster processors are available at a greater price. As a general rule, if you are intending to use your computer for tasks such as word processing, desktop publishing, keeping accounts and records, sending and receiving e-mails and searching the Internet, then a basic processor of perhaps 1 or 2GHz will be quite good enough.

It's not necessary for the general user to keep up with all the latest offerings from the processor manufacturers. For example, one of my machines has a relatively out-of-date 1GHz processor but this is quite adequate for the sort of tasks listed above and the word processing and DTP tasks described in detail later in this book.

If you later find that you need a more powerful processor, it may be possible to "upgrade" your existing computer. Check before buying a new system whether the processor can be upgraded at a later date. It may simply be a case of unplugging the old processor and replacing it with the new one. This is much cheaper than buying a new computer.

You don't need the latest "gee-whiz" computer – you can do impressive word processing and DTP work with any PC machine bought in the last few years.

The Memory

The memory (also known as RAM or Random Access Memory) is a set of microchips which act as a store for the data or information typed in at the keyboard. The memory also holds the programs that you are currently using. The memory is only a *temporary store*. Like the processor, the size of the memory can have a major effect on the performance of the computer. Modern programs, with all of their graphics, windows and icons, demand massive amounts of memory. Photographs are also memory hungry.

If your computer is short of memory, programs will run very slowly. Therefore it's best to buy a computer with as much memory as possible. Currently machines are being sold with 256 or 512MB of memory. If buying a new machine, aim for at least 256MB to start off with. Memory is usually relatively cheap, although prices do fluctuate. It's a 10 minute job to plug extra memory into the computer at a later date. Expect to pay around £20-£30 for the extra memory or RAM chips, also known as SIMMs.

Please note: Memory is Volatile

Any data (text, photographs, etc.) stored in the memory during a computing session is lost as soon as the computer is switched off. Any data you wish to keep must be saved on a magnetic storage medium such as your hard disc drive, discussed shortly.

(The term MB above stands for Megabyte. This is roughly a million *bytes* – one byte being the amount of memory or disc space needed to store a *character*. A character is a letter of the alphabet, a digit 0-9, or a punctuation mark – in fact, most of the keys on a keyboard).

The Hard Disc Drive

The hard disc drive is a sealed unit built inside of the computer. You won't normally see your hard disc drive unless you remove the computer's metal casing. The magnetic disc surfaces on which programs and data are recorded are an integral part of the drive unit, which also contains the heads used for reading and writing data.

The hard disc is usually designated as the **C:** drive, and consists of a set of metal discs, coated in a magnetic material and rotating at high speed about a central spindle. This makes it very fast at saving and retrieving data.

The amount of data which can be stored on a hard disc is normally measured in *gigabytes* (*GB*). A gigabyte is roughly 1000 megabytes (discussed earlier in this chapter). At the time of writing computers are being supplied with 80-200GB of hard disc storage.

The Contents of the Hard Disc Drive

The hard disc inside of the computer is like the filing cabinet in a traditional office. When you switch the computer off, the contents of the hard disc remain in place. The hard disc normally contains:

- The *systems software* such as the Windows XP operating system needed to start and run the computer. This may be pre-installed on a new computer or installed later from the Windows CD.

- The *applications software* (programs) such as your word processor, database, desktop publishing (DTP) and Internet browser. This may be included on a new machine or bought as a separate package and installed from the CD provided. Instructions pop up on the screen after placing the CD in the drive.

- The work you have produced by entering text at the keyboard and perhaps including pictures and photographs. Documents saved on the hard disc are known as *files*. You need to save a document on the hard disc as soon as it has been entered at the keyboard. A long document should be saved at regular intervals, each new version "overwriting" the previous one on the hard disc. This can be set to happen automatically every few minutes, say.

Always Back Up Important Documents

Although hard discs are very reliable, it is possible to lose your work by accidentally deleting the wrong files.

Always make regular backup copies of important documents on a separate magnetic storage medium, such as a CD-R or one of the removable mini drives which plug into a USB port on the computer.

The Printer

A reliable printer is an essential part of your word processing system – it's not yet possible to do everything by e-mail or posting on Web sites. A printer is needed to produce paper copies of letters, reports, publications, magazines, photographs, e-mails and Web pages.

Nowadays there are two popular types of printer used in the home and small business. These are the *inkjet* and the *laser printer*. You need to consider the type of work you will be doing in order to choose a suitable printer.

The Inkjet Printer

Inkjet printers are good all-rounders and can be bought for as little as £50, although models costing several hundred pounds are also available. High quality documents can be produced using a word processor and cheap inkjet printer.

You must also consider the price of the ink cartridges (both black and colour) which can cost from £10-£20 or more. Inkjet printers can produce high quality colour photographs, though the cost of the cartridges and the special glossy paper makes this an expensive activity.

The Laser Printer

Laser printers are popular in business. They are fast, produce high quality printout and tend to be quieter than inkjets. At one time most laser printers were *mono,* i.e. they printed only in black and white. Until recently colour laser printers were too expensive for home use, costing thousands of pounds. At the time of writing mono laser printers can be bought for less than £100, while the colour versions now cost from about £250 upwards.

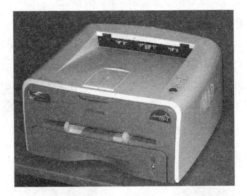

Laser printers use a powder called *toner* as their "ink" and the toner cartridges must be replaced periodically. A new laser toner cartridge may typically cost around £50, but this may be capable of printing several thousand sheets of A4 paper.

The Dot Matrix Printer

Dot matrix printers used to be popular as they are quite fast and can print on continuous rolls of paper. The dot-matrix printer is suitable for producing large quantities of documents where high quality text is not essential, such as address labels and invoices and delivery notes.

The Scanner

The scanner is a desirable extra rather than an essential part of a word processing system. A popular version is the A4 flatbed scanner, a flat box roughly the size of a large folder, as shown on the right. Scanners cost from about £50 upwards.

Using a scanner, an image of a piece of paper containing text and/or graphics can be copied and inserted into a document on the screen. Alternatively the scanned image can be saved on your hard disc or sent to a range of destinations such as e-mail or the Web. As shown from the following menu (for an Epson scanner), the scanner can also copy a document straight to your printer.

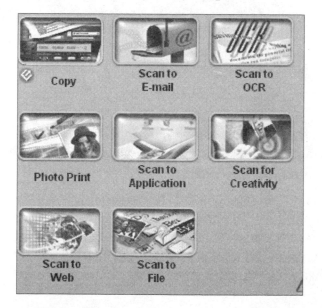

Giving New Life to Old Photographs

The scanner is useful for copying (or "digitizing") existing paper documents and incorporating them into a word processing page. Shown below is an image which has been scanned from an old family photograph. Once the image is in the computer it can be saved as a file on the hard disc and inserted into a word processing page such as this one.

Inexpensive software such as Paint Shop Pro and Adobe Photoshop Elements allows you to improve images copied from old photographs, e.g. to remove scratches or damage.

New Photographs

Nowadays photographs can be taken with a digital camera and input directly into a computer using a special cable, as discussed shortly. The images can then be edited and enhanced on the screen, inserted into documents or printed on glossy photographic paper using an inkjet printer.

The Digital Camera

A digital camera will enable you to add your own photographs to enhance your word processing documents. First you take a photograph with a digital camera. Then you transfer the image to your computer and save it on the hard disc. Next the photograph can be polished up in a program like Paint Shop Pro or Adobe Photoshop Elements. A copy of the photograph can be included on the page of a word processing document; for example, to illustrate an advert or poster or to add interest to a letter to friends and family. As discussed later, the position and size of the photograph can be adjusted to give the best page result.

Cheap digital cameras can be bought for as little as £40, while better quality ones may cost several hundred pounds. The digital camera doesn't use film, but instead has a memory card. The images are stored in the memory until you "download" them to your computer. This is done by connecting the camera to the computer using a special cable as shown below.

Once your photographs have been safely stored on your hard disc, the memory card in the camera can be "wiped" ready to be used again for your next batch of photographs.

This subject is discussed in detail in our previous book:

Digital Photography and Computing

for the Older Generation

Bernard Babani (publishing) Ltd.

The Internet Connection

It is essential nowadays for your home office to be connected to the Internet. In a word processing context, you could use the Internet in many ways, including:

- Sending a large word processing document as an e-mail *attachment*. I have sent whole chapters of books to the printers in this way. In order to send larger documents such as a complete book, for example, you really need a broadband Internet connection rather than the much slower traditional "56K modem" (discussed shortly).

- Sending e-mails to colleagues or friends, perhaps to liaise about a word processing project such as a local magazine or report.

- Using the Internet to research material for any sort of word processing document or report. The scope of the Internet in providing information on any subject, no matter how obscure, is incredible. It is also a rich source of information on topics such as family history and parish records.

There are two basic types of Internet connection:

- The traditional connection which uses a small box called a *56K modem* or *dial-up modem* to connect your computer to the Internet via the telephone lines.

- The newer system, known as *broadband*, which connects your computer to the Internet using a device called an *ADSL modem*.

The initial cost of the modem and other equipment may be under £100 or even free in some cases. The main cost is your subscription to your Internet Service Provider – a company such as AOL, Tiscali or BT.

The broadband system is more expensive, currently around £16 - £25 per month compared with much less for the 56K system.

If you can afford it, the broadband system has some important advantages. It is much faster, allowing you to send and receive large word processing documents and other files much more quickly. In addition you can use the Internet at the same time as a telephone handset connected to the same telephone line. This is sometimes helpful if you are talking to someone on the telephone but need to refer to something on the computer screen. For example, a member of a telephone support team can talk you through a technical problem, giving you instructions via the telephone while you carry them out on the computer; or you might want to talk to a friend about a Web page currently on the computer screen. This is made possible by a broadband component known as a *filter* which divides a single telephone line into two; one line for the broadband Internet and another line for normal telephone use.

Networking

If you have more than one computer you may wish to connect them to form a network. This will allow several computers to share a single Internet connection and also exchange files between computers. In order to network the computers you need a device called a *router*. This allows the computers to be connected together by cables or in a wireless network as discussed earlier in this chapter.

Glossary of Computing Terms

Application

A program used to perform a particular task such as word processing. New application software is installed on the hard disc (from a CD) then "launched" whenever required.

Attachment

A file such as a word processing document can be "clipped" to an e-mail message. Then it can be sent and received electronically along with the e-mail message.

Base Unit

The metal box containing most of the essential components of the computer.

Broadband

The latest technology used to connect a computer to the Internet via the telephone network. Very much faster than the earlier system known as "dial-up" or "56K modem".

CD/DVD Drive

A small box which allows CDs and DVDs to be read and (on some drives) to be created. Also called a Combo Unit.

CD-R

A cheap form of storage suitable for making backup copies of your work. The CD-R can only be recorded on once.

CD-RW

A CD which can be used for recording many times.

CRT

A type of monitor or screen based on the Cathode Ray Tube; many new computers use the much slimmer TFT monitor, which is more expensive but saves desk space.

Dial-up Modem

A device for connecting a computer to the Internet. The dial-up modem (also known as the 56K modem) is rapidly being superseded by much faster broadband systems.

Digital Camera

A camera which stores images on a memory card rather than a film. The images are transferred to a computer where they can be edited, printed or inserted into documents.

DVD Drive

A small box in the computer which allows video discs to be viewed; some DVD drives also allow videos to be created on a blank disc.

Expansion Card

A small circuit board plugged inside of a computer to provide functions such as sound and graphics capability. Some modems are available as expansion cards.

File

Documents saved on disc are known as files or sometimes data files. Software or programs installed on a hard disc are often known as program files or *applications*.

Gigabyte (GB)

A measure of the storage capacity of a hard disc. One gigabyte is approximately 1000 megabytes.

Gigahertz (GHz)

A measure of the speed of a computer processor.

Hard Disc Drive

A magnetic disc fixed inside the computer. Used to store your work and the software needed to run the computer and to carry out applications such as word processing.

Icon

A small picture on the screen representing a program or action which can be launched by pointing and "clicking" with the mouse.

Inkjet Printer

A popular printer used in the home and small business to print colour and black and white documents and photographs.

Laser Printer

A fast and quiet printer which uses toner powder to produce high quality documents. Colour laser printers are relatively expensive.

Magnifier

A feature of the Microsoft Windows operating system that allows parts of the screen to be enlarged to help people with impaired vision.

Megabyte (MB)

A measure of storage capacity, usually applied to the computer's memory. One megabyte is capable of storing roughly 1 million characters (letters, digits 0-9, etc.)

Memory

A set of chips plugged into the computer and used to store the current program and also data – e.g. the text of your word processing document. The memory is cleared when the computer is switched off.

Modem

A device for connecting a computer to the Internet via the telephone lines. The traditional dial-up or 56K modem is currently being superseded by faster broadband systems.

Monitor

The screen used to view your work. Traditional monitors are based on the Cathode Ray Tube technology while much slimmer TFT monitors are becoming very popular,

Motherboard

The main circuit board inside of a computer containing the processor and memory chips and connections to all of the main components. Some functions such as sound and graphics can be supplied "on board" the motherboard or plugged in as separate expansion cards.

Mouse

A small device used to move a pointer over objects on the screen. A button on the mouse is "clicked" over an object to initiate a particular action.

Network

A network is formed when two or more computers are connected to exchange data files or share an Internet connection. Traditional networks have used cables to connect machines, while wireless "WI-FI" networks are becoming popular.

PC

The name given to a Personal Computer which conforms to the ubiquitous IBM-compatible standard. PCs can all run the same software, usually written for the Microsoft Windows operating system.

Processor

The main chip which carries out all of the instructions in programs – often called the "brains" of the computer.

QWERTY

The name given to the standard keyboard, based on the layout of the first six letter keys.

Resolution

A measure of the coarseness or otherwise of the screen display, usually measured in *pixels* – the small *picture elements* which make up an image. Common screen resolutions are 800x600 and 1024x768.

Scanner

A device which allows paper documents to be copied into a computer's memory, where they can be edited or inserted into other documents.

TFT

A very slim type of monitor which uses "Thin Film Transistor" technology. Useful for saving desk space.

Tower Unit

A vertical box containing all of the main components of the computer; often situated on the floor to save desk space.

USB Port

One of several small rectangular slots usually on the back of the computer, allowing peripheral devices such as printers, scanners, digital cameras, etc., to be connected.

Wireless (WI-FI) Network

A method of connecting computers using radio signals, rather than cables, for the sharing of data files and an Internet connection.

Writing

The process of recording data and programs on a magnetic disc such as the hard disc or a recordable CD.

Working With Windows XP

What is Windows XP?

Familiarity with Microsoft Windows is essential if you are to manage your word processing activities efficiently. Windows XP is the latest in a line of Microsoft Windows operating systems and controls tasks such as:

- Displaying the Startup screen, known as the Windows Desktop

- Controlling windows and icons on the screen and making selections from menus with a mouse

- Starting programs such as the word processor

- Saving your work as a file on your hard disc

- Organising your work into a system of folders and deleting unwanted and obsolete files

- Printing documents on paper or sending them as e-mail attachments

- Connecting to the Internet

- Managing devices such as scanners, printers, etc.

- Shutting down the computer in a safe fashion.

The Windows Desktop

The Windows **Desktop** appears at the end of the startup process, displaying the **Start** button in the bottom left-hand corner and the Windows **TaskBar** along the bottom, as shown in the screenshot below.

Down the left-hand side of the desktop are icons representing various programs. These icons are often called *shortcuts* since you can start a program by simply double-clicking its icon with the mouse, instead of going through a system of menus. Shortcuts are often placed on the desktop automatically when you install a new piece of software. Alternatively you can create your own shortcuts, as discussed later. You can also create a shortcut on the desktop to open up a folder containing your current work. For example I have created a desktop shortcut to a folder containing all of the chapters of this book

The **Start** menu shown below is launched by clicking on the **Start** button at the bottom left of the desktop.

Frequently-used programs such as the Microsoft Word word processor are automatically placed in the **Start** menu.

Simply click the name of the program or its icon to launch the program, as shown on the right,  ready to start a word processing session.

The **Start** menu also displays the **Turn Off Computer** button for shutting down the computer safely, before you switch off the  power. Always use the **Turn Off Computer** button to end a word processing session. Simply switching off the power will cause work to be lost and may cause other problems.

My Documents shown above right, is a special folder in which your work is saved "by default", unless you specify a different folder. (Creating your own folders and saving your work is discussed later). As shown below, apart from the documents and files you save, **My Documents** can also contain saved copies of pictures, music and e-books.

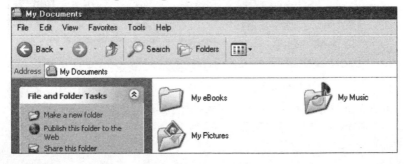

If you select **My Recent Documents** as shown on the previous menu, you are presented with a list of the latest documents you have been working on. Some recent documents are listed on the right of the following extract from the **Start** menu.

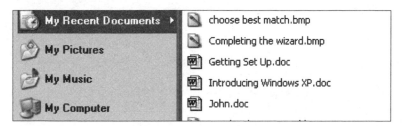

Please note that in this context a "document" is not just a letter or report in a word processor. Drawings and paintings, for example are also referred to as documents.

Also note that when a document is saved as a file, a file name is given by the user. For example, I have named a letter as **John** above. Then Windows has automatically added **.doc** to indicate that this is a word processing document. These *file name* *extensions* can be switched on and off in the Windows Explorer by selecting **Tools**, **Folder Options...**, **View** and **Hide extensions for known file types**. Then select **Apply** and **OK**. The document is further identified by the icon for a word processing document, shown right. A picture is saved with a different icon and a file name extension such as **.bmp,** which stands for Windows "bitmap". There are several other file name extensions for pictures and these are discussed later in this book.

The feature **My Recent Documents** provides a quick way of calling up a document you have recently been working on.

My Computer

Referring to the extract from the **Start** menu shown below, **My Computer** listed in the right-hand panel is a very important tool used in the management of your computer

Clicking **My Computer** in the above **Start** menu brings up the window shown below.

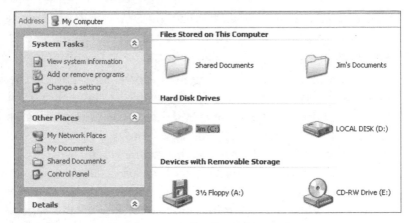

My Computer allows you to look at the various resources on your computer, such as disc drives and CDs. Amongst other things, you can carry out maintenance tasks such as

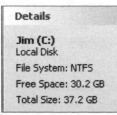

cleaning up your hard disc by deleting unwanted files. When you click on the icon for the hard disc drive as shown above, the panel at the bottom left of the **My Computer** window shows the amount of free hard disc space.

The Windows Explorer

To start the Windows Explorer, click the *right-hand* mouse button over the **Start** button at the bottom left of the screen. A menu pops up from which you click **Explore**.

The Windows Explorer is one of the main ways to locate a piece of work such as a word processing document (also called a file). Then the document can be opened in the program which created it. The Windows Explorer lists all of the resources of your computer (disc drives, folders, sub-folders, etc.) in a list down the left-hand side of the screen, as shown below.

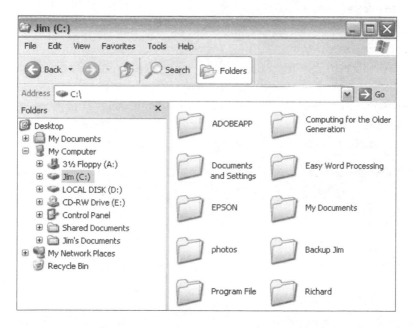

The right-hand panel on the previous page shows the contents of any discs or folders you have selected by clicking with the mouse. You can carry out a variety of management tasks on the folders and files listed in Explorer by right-clicking over the appropriate file or folder name or icon. This produces a menu as shown on the right.

Easy Word Processing
Explore
Open
Search...
Scan Folders for Viruses

Send To   ▶

Cut
Copy

Create Shortcut
Delete
Rename

Properties

Amongst other things, the menu includes options to copy, delete, rename and create a shortcut to a file or folder from the Windows XP Desktop.

The Windows Explorer has a Menu Bar across the top with several drop-down menus. For example, to change the way the folders and files are displayed in the right-hand panel, click **View**. The **View** menu drops down allowing you to display the folders in various ways including **Thumbnails**, **Icons, Tiles, Icons**, as a **List** and with all **Details**. In the example below, the icons are displayed in the **Tiles** view.

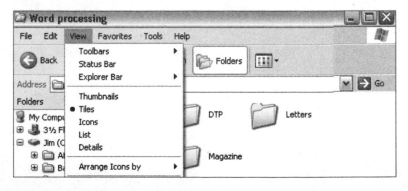

Creating Your Own System of Folders

Suppose you want to create your own system of folders in the Windows Explorer in order to keep your work in an organized fashion. Then you can find a document straightaway, avoiding the frequently heard cry "The stupid computer has lost all my work!" A possible system of folders stored on the **C:** drive (the hard disc) might be as follows.

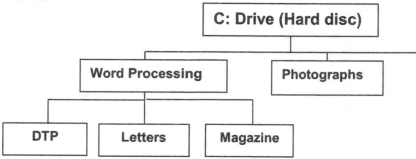

In the above diagram, I have decided to create a folder called **Word Processing** on the **C:** drive. This will hold all of my word processing documents in three sub-folders, **DTP**, **Letters** and **Magazine**.

When this "filing system" is set up in the Windows Explorer it looks like this:

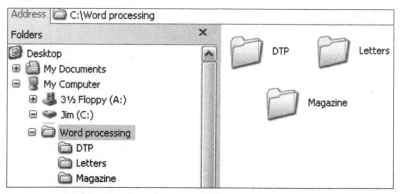

Please note in the left-hand panel on the previous page, a **+** sign next to a folder means there are sub-folders within. Click the **+** sign to open the folder. A **−** sign now appears next to the open folder. The contents of the open folder appear in the right-hand panel of Windows Explorer as shown on the previous page. Click the **−** sign to close the folder.

In Windows Explorer you can display the details of saved documents by selecting **View** and **Details**. In the example below I have saved a file called **Letter to council** in my **Letters** folder, all within the **Word Processing** folder on the **C:** drive.

Name ▲	Size	Type	Date Modified
📝 Letter to council	24 KB	Microsoft Word Doc...	09/05/2005 15:39

You can also display the file **Letter to council** as an icon as shown below by selecting **View** and **Icons** from the Menu Bar in the Windows Explorer.

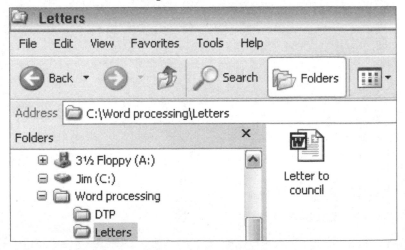

Launching Programs

We have seen that frequently-used programs can be started from the left-hand side of the **Start** menu and also from *shortcut icons* on the Windows XP Desktop. Many programs, however, are launched by selecting **Start** and **All Programs**, as shown below.

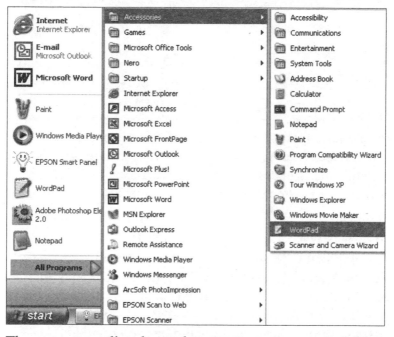

The programs listed on the **All Programs** menu shown above are a mixture of the software applications you have installed (such as Microsoft Word or Works) and also the programs included within Windows XP itself.

The **Accessories** menu shown above includes two simple word processing programs, **Notepad** and **WordPad** and also **Paint**, a drawing and painting program which can be used to create illustrations for word processing documents.

Accessibility Features

Windows XP allows you to set up a number of **Accessibility** features to help with people with impaired vision, hearing and mobility. These features are listed after selecting **Accessibility** from the **Accessories** menu.

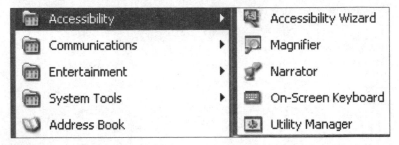

Please note that, as in the case of the **Accessibility Wizard** shown above, a **Wizard** is a program which guides you through the process of setting up a piece of hardware or software. The **Accessibility** features are discussed in more detail later in this book.

System Tools

An important feature within the **Accessories** menu is **System Tools**, shown below. This menu includes a number of maintenance tools intended to keep your computer running efficiently, such as **Disk Cleanup**, and **Disk Defragmenter**. These tools should be used regularly.

The Control Panel

This is an essential component of Windows XP, used (amongst other things) for altering settings and adding and removing new hardware and software. The **Control Panel** can be launched by clicking its name in the previously shown **Start** menu. Alternatively click **Change a setting** in the **System Tasks** menu on the left of the **My Computer** window. The **Control Panel** opens in the **Category View** shown below. This view shows the tasks, under broad headings, which can be performed using the **Control Panel**.

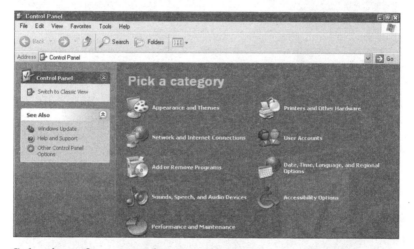

Selecting, for example, **Performance and Maintenance** as shown above, leads to some more specific tasks for you to choose from, as follows:

→ Adjust visual effects

→ Free up space on your hard disk

→ Back up your data

→ Rearrange items on your hard disk to make programs run faster

The Control Panel in Classic View

Earlier versions of Windows showed the Control Panel as a set of icons representing the various tools. This arrangement, now known as **Classic View**, is still available in Windows XP. **Classic View** can be selected by clicking the option **Switch to Classic View** in the Control Panel in **Category View** shown previously.

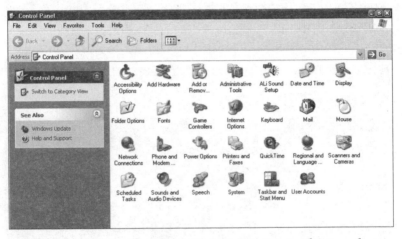

With the Control Panel in **Classic View**, as shown above, changes are made to settings after double-clicking the appropriate icon. For example, double-clicking the **Display** icon allows you to change all of your screen colours and to select a *screen saver*.

A screen saver is a display which occupies your screen if the computer is not used for a few minutes. The screen saver presents a constantly changing pattern or picture. This is to prevent burning of the monitor which might occur if the display remained fixed for a long time. There is a choice of screen savers within Windows XP and many others are available in all sorts of designs.

Windows Update

Both views of the Control Panel also give access to **Windows Update**. Clicking this option connects your computer to the Internet (if your machine already has a modem set up to connect to the Internet.) Here you are given the opportunity to

download the latest upgrades available for the Windows software installed on your computer. (*Downloading* means transferring files, i.e. programs and data, from the Internet to your computer).

Deleting Files - The Recycle Bin

This is a container for your deleted files and folders. When you delete a file by pressing the **Delete** key over the file name in the Windows Explorer or My Computer, the file is initially sent to the **Recycle Bin**. Files and folders in the **Recycle Bin** are still taking up space on your hard disc.

The **Recycle Bin** is launched by double-clicking its icon on

the Windows XP Desktop. From here the files can be permanently deleted. Alternatively, files in the **Recycle Bin** which have not yet been permanently deleted can still be restored to their original location on the hard disc.

That completes the tour of the main features of the Windows XP operating system. The next section looks at the different parts of a window and how we use them.

Windows and Mice

Windows are rectangular boxes on the screen, used to frame the current task.

A window might contain, for example:

- A document in an *application* such as a word processor, drawing program or a spreadsheet

- A display of discs and folders in My Computer or the Windows Explorer

- The set of icons or a list of tasks in the Control Panel, used for setting up hardware and software.

Although windows are used for such diverse purposes, in general they contain the same basic components. Shortly we will look at the make-up of a typical window. However, since the mouse plays a central role in the operation of windows, let's look at the use of the mouse in some detail.

You can tailor the mouse and pointer to work in the way you prefer. Select **Start, Control Panel** and make sure you are displaying **Classic View**. Double-click the mouse icon, shown on the right, to make various adjustments to the way the mouse and pointer work. These include swapping the functions of the left and right buttons and altering the double-click speed.

(As discussed elsewhere in this book, many operations can be carried out by simultaneously pressing certain combinations of keys, as an alternative to using the mouse. For example, **Ctrl+P** causes a document to be printed on paper. **Ctrl+P** means, literally, while holding down the key marked **Ctrl**, press the **P** key.)

Mouse Operations

Click

This means a single press of the left mouse button. With the cursor over an icon or screen object, a click will cause, for example, a command from a menu to be carried out or a folder to open.

Double-Click

This means pressing the left mouse button very quickly twice in succession. This is often used to carry out operations such as starting a program from an icon on the Windows Desktop. Folders can be set to open with either a single or double-click (discussed later).

Right-Click

Pressing the right button while the pointer is over a screen object is a quick way to open up additional menus relating to the object. For example, if you right-click over the **Start** button on the Taskbar, a menu appears giving, amongst other things, a quick way to start the Windows Explorer.

Open
Browse With Paint Shop Pro 7
Explore
Search...
Properties

Dragging and Dropping

This is used to move objects about the screen. This includes moving files and folders into different folders or disc drives. Click over the object, then, keeping the left button held down, move the mouse pointer (together with the object) to the new position. Release the left button to place the object in its new position. Dragging is also used to resize windows and graphics on the screen.

Windows in Detail

The parts of a window can be illustrated using My Computer or the Windows Explorer. **My Computer** is selected from the **Start** menu. The Explorer can be launched by *right-clicking* over the **Start** button and then clicking **Explore** on the menu which appears.

In this example I have clicked on a folder called **Home** and then on a sub-folder called **Holidays**.

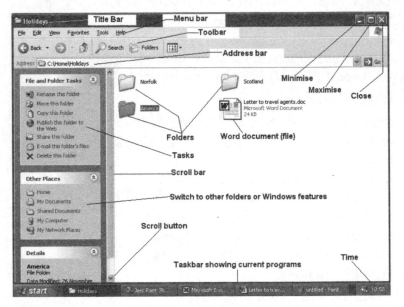

Similar windows are used for different purposes in Windows XP. For example, if you were word processing in Microsoft Word, your document on the screen would be contained in a window with a Title Bar, Menu Bar, Toolbar and Taskbar. Both vertical and horizontal Scroll Bars may be displayed at different times.

You can choose which Toolbars are displayed by switching them on or off after selecting **View** and **Toolbars**.

Next, consider the three heavily used buttons in the top right of the screen, Maximize, Minimize and Resize.

The Maximise Button

Click this to make the window fill the entire screen.

The Minimise Button

Click this to reduce the window to an icon on the Taskbar at the bottom of the screen as shown below.

Letter to hotel.doc - ...   untitled - Paint   Microsoft Excel - Bo...

The Taskbar above shows that the computer is currently running three programs. These are:

- A document, **Letter to hotel.doc**, open in Word.
- A drawing in Microsoft Paint.
- A spreadsheet in Microsoft Excel

Click the icon on the Taskbar to restore a minimised window back to its original size. The icon on the Taskbar can also be clicked to minimise an open window.

The Restore Button

After a window has been maximised, the Maximise Button is replaced by the Restore Button shown right. Clicking this reduces the window to its original size.

Closing a Window

To shut down the current window, click the Close Button, marked with a cross, in the top right-hand corner of the screen.

Resizing a Window

You can change the size of a window by dragging arrows on each of the four sides and in the corners of the window. Move the mouse pointer over the border until the arrows appear. Then drag the border to the required size.

The Menu Bar

The Menu Bar is a list of words across the top of the window starting with **File, Edit** and **View**, etc. For example, the menu bar from the Microsoft Word program is shown below. The icons underneath the Menu Bar are the Toolbar.

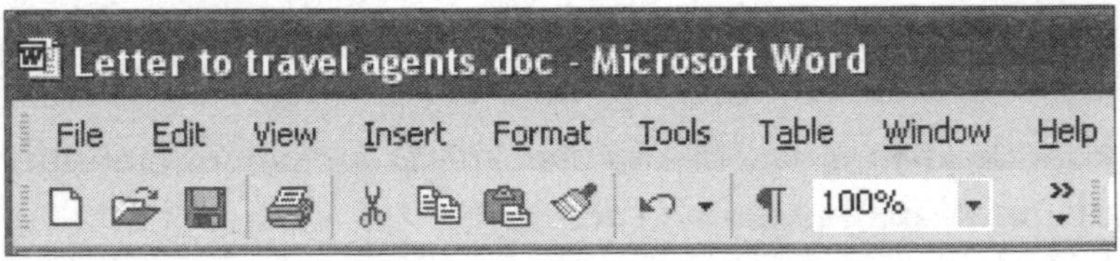

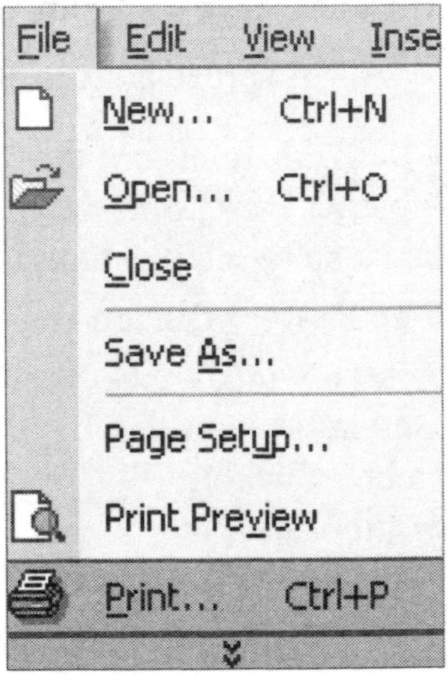

A single click of a word on the Menu Bar reveals a drop-down menu, such as the **File** menu illustrated. Then the required command is executed, again with a single click. Clicking the two small arrows at the bottom of the drop-down menu shown on the right extends the list of options.

Windows programs in general have a similar Menu Bar with the options **File, Edit** and **View**, etc., although there are some differences in individual programs.

The row of icons under the Menu Bar is part of the Standard Toolbar in Word. Similar Toolbars appear in other programs.

 Allow the pointer to dwell over an icon. After a second or so a note appears describing the function of the icon. For example, when you hover over the scissors icon, the **Cut** command is revealed as shown on the left. This is used to delete or cut a piece of text in a document. (First you must highlight or select the required text by dragging with the mouse).

You can switch various toolbars on and off after selecting **View** and **Toolbars** from the Menu Bar as shown in the following example from Word.

Print Layout		✓	Standard
Toolbars	▶	✓	Formatting
Header and Footer			AutoText
Zoom...			Control Toolbox
⌄			Database
A		✓	Drawing
m			

Displaying Two or More Windows at a Time

When two or more programs are running at the same time, normally only one of them is seen in a window on the screen. However, it is sometimes useful to display two or more windows on the screen simultaneously; for example, when "cutting and pasting" text or pictures from one document to another. This can be achieved after *right-clicking* on an *empty part* of the Windows Taskbar at the bottom of the screen. Shown below is a Window displaying a photograph in the image editor Adobe Photoshop Elements. The right-hand window shows the same image copied into the word processor Microsoft Word. This was achieved by selecting **Tile Windows Vertically** when running Word and Adobe Photoshop Elements simultaneously.

Toolbars	▶
Cascade Windows	
Tile Windows Horizontally	
Tile Windows Vertically	
Show the Desktop	
Task Manager	

Image Editor   **Word Processor**

The **Cascade Windows** option shown in the menu on the previous page has the effect of arranging the windows on top of each other in layers, but with the Title Bar of each window clearly visible. Clicking on the Title Bar of a window brings that window to the top layer.

Dialogue Boxes

Whereas the windows discussed previously contain running programs and folders, *dialogue boxes* (as shown below) usually require the user to enter information or specify settings. (Microsoft Windows provides *default* settings and names which will usually suffice until you are ready to insert your own settings.)

Dialogue boxes appear after you select a menu command which ends in an ellipsis (**...**) such as **Save As...** and **Print...**. The **Print** dialogue box shown below contains many of the most common features of dialogue boxes.

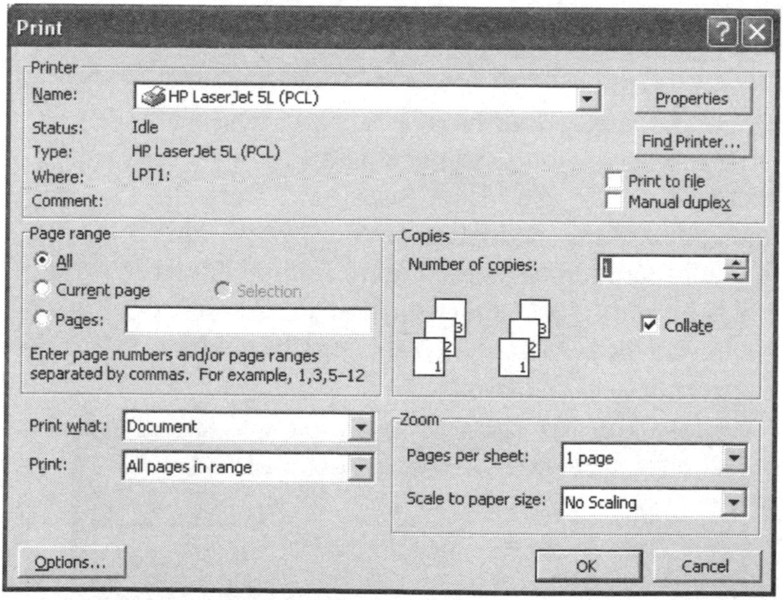

The white circles under **Page range** on the previous dialogue box are known as *radio buttons*, switched on or off with a single click. Only one of a group of radio buttons can be switched on at a given time.

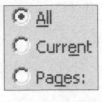

The white squares next to **Print to file**, **Manual duplex** and **Collate** are known as *check boxes*. Any number of check boxes can be switched on or off at a given time.

Clicking the *down arrow* on the right of a horizontal bar reveals a *drop-down menu* of choices, such as several printers, as shown below.

HP LaserJet 5L (PCL)	▼
Acrobat Distiller	
Acrobat PDFWriter	
EPSON Stylus C60 Series	
Generic PostScript Printer	
HP LaserJet 5L	
HP LaserJet 5L (PCL)	

Some dialogue boxes have a *text bar* which allows you to type in your own words, such as a file or folder name. For example, when you select **Save As...** from the **File** menu, the **Save As...** dialogue box appears. This includes an icon to create a new folder, shown on the right. Click this icon and then enter a name for the new folder in the text box which appears, as shown below.

New Folder

Name: [   ]

OK
Cancel

Creating a Shortcut Icon on the Desktop

To provide a shortcut icon on the Windows Desktop for any of your programs, from the **Start** menu select **All Programs**. *Right-click* the name or icon for the program and then click **Send To**. Now select **Desktop (create shortcut)** to place an icon on the Windows Desktop.

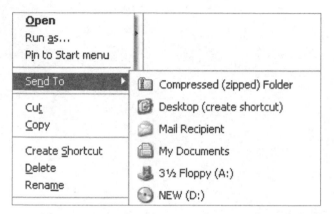

You can also create shortcuts to frequently used files and folders on the desktop. Right-click over the file or folder in the Windows Explorer, then select **Send To** and **Desktop (create shortcut)** as before.

Please note that you can also use the above method of right-clicking a file or folder to make a copy to a floppy disc or CD. Simply select the appropriate media, as shown in the menu above. In this example **NEW (D:)** represents the CD drive. As discussed later, this method is useful for making backup copies of important work.

Compressed (zipped) Folder shown above is a feature of Windows XP which stores files (such as word processing documents) in a very compact format, saving disc space.

Shown below are some shortcut icons on my Windows Desktop which are relevant in the context of this book.

Double-clicking the shortcut icon for a *program* causes the program to be launched, i.e. started up. In the case of a shortcut icon for a *folder*, double-clicking the folder's icon opens the folder in the Windows Explorer.

The icons shown above are shortcuts to the Microsoft Word word processor, the Adobe Photoshop Elements program for editing images and the popular Google Internet search program or "search engine". Google is extremely useful for searching for any sort of information, such as material for a word processing document or report.

Microsoft Works shown above is a suite of programs including a word processor very closely related to Microsoft Word. The **Shortcut to Easy Word Processing** above opens up a folder containing files representing the chapters of this book. The **Recycle Bin** is a receptacle for any files you may have deleted in the Windows Explorer.

Help for Users With Special Needs

Introduction

Microsoft Windows XP contains a number of features to help users with impairments in any of the following:

- Vision
- Hearing
- Mobility.

The special needs features in Windows XP are fairly basic and some users with special needs may require more specialised accessibility software. However, the tools included in Windows XP are free and should help some users with special needs with their word processing activities. The features are launched by selecting **Start, All Programs, Accessories** and **Accessibility**.

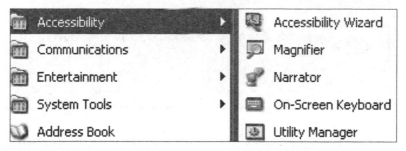

The next section looks at the five **Accessibility** options, shown in the right-hand panel above.

The Accessibility Wizard

A wizard is a program which leads you through a series of interactive screens. The user makes selections from various choices before clicking **Next** to move on to the next screen. Wizards are frequently used in Microsoft Windows for setting up new hardware and software.

Start the **Accessibility Wizard** by clicking **Start, All Programs, Accessories** and **Accessibility**. First you see the **Accessibility Welcome Screen** and on clicking **Next** you are given the option to select a larger text size.

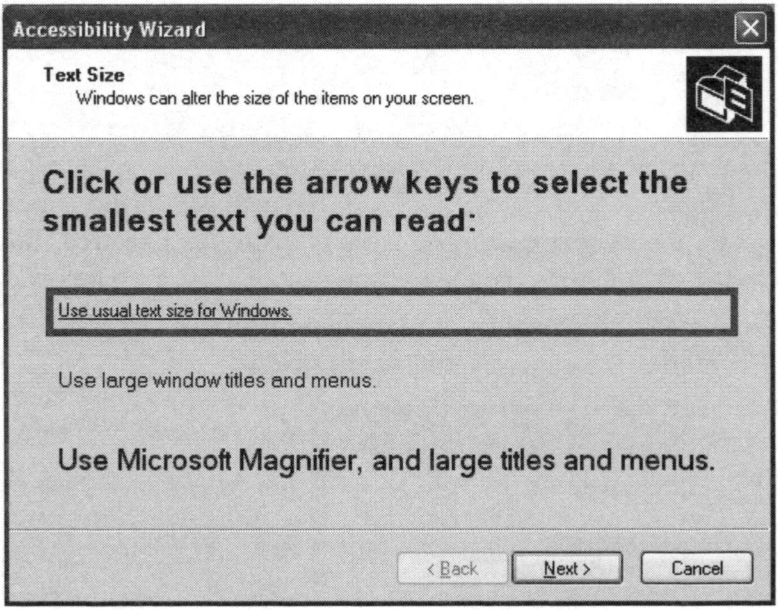

Further dialogue boxes in the wizard allow you to increase the text size which appears in windows title bars and also to increase the size of scroll bars.

Then you are asked to specify your own special needs, by ticking the check boxes for conditions which apply to you.

The Accessibility Wizard then proceeds in one of several ways, depending on the ticks you have placed in the above check boxes. For example, if your vision is impaired, the option to display large icons is presented, as shown below.

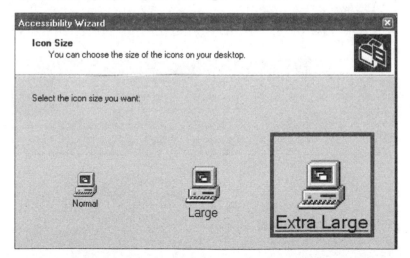

Another dialogue box allows you to select a high contrast colour display and this is followed by a box giving a choice of various colours and sizes of *mouse cursor*.

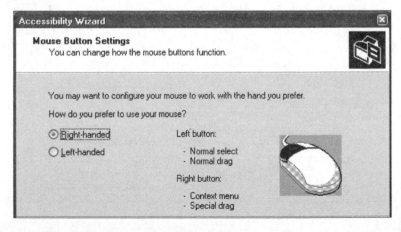

If you have difficulty using a mouse, the numeric keypad on the right of the keyboard can be used instead. For example, the cursor can be controlled by the arrow keys, a mouse-click is replaced by pressing the number **5** key and double-clicking is replaced by the + key. Finally a dialogue box appears allowing you to swap the function of the left and right mouse buttons, to work with your preferred hand.

After completing all of the dialogue boxes, click **Finish** to leave the Accessibility Wizard. Please note that you can also set the **Accessibility Options** without using the Wizard. First enter the **Control Panel** from the **Start** menu. Make sure the **Control Panel** is in **Classic View**. If the **Control Panel** is currently in **Category View**, click **Switch to Classic View** from the top left-hand corner of the **Control Panel**.

Now double-click the icon for **Accessibility Options**. The following dialogue box opens. A series of tabs (**Keyboard, Sound, Display,** etc.) give access to many further options.

The Magnifier

This feature enables the person with impaired vision to enlarge different areas of the screen, as required. The Magnifier is started by clicking **Start**, **All Programs**, **Accessories**, **Accessibility** and **Magnifier**, as shown below.

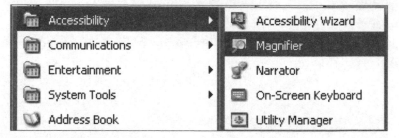

A settings dialogue box also appears, giving you the option to change the magnification level in the range 1 to 9.

You are presented with a note stating that the Magnifier is intended for users with slight visual impairment. Those with more serious visual problems may need a program with higher functionality.

Note in the dialogue box on the previous page, you can set the magnifier to follow the mouse cursor and the keyboard focus. You can also invert colours to make the screen easier to read. The magnifier appears in its own window above the normal screen. As you move about the normal screen, the magnifier tracks the cursor or keyboard and displays the local text and graphics enlarged, as if viewed through a magnifying glass. Shown below is a screenshot from Microsoft Word, with the magnifier running. The area of the screen around the current position is shown magnified across the top of the screen.

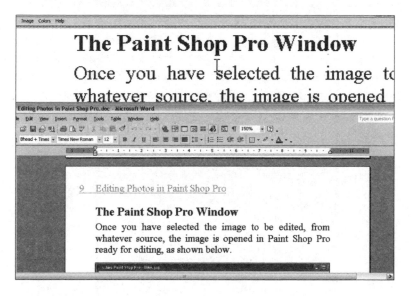

The Narrator

If your computer is fitted with a sound card and speakers, the Narrator can read out the text in menus and describe features such as buttons in dialogue boxes. The Narrator can also read out the letters and keys pressed as you type them into a document. To start the program, select **Start**, **All Programs**, **Accessories**, **Accessibility** and **Narrator**.

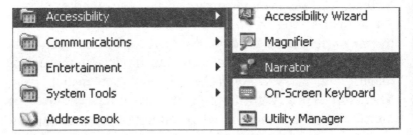

After clicking **Narrator**, an introductory window appears informing you that **Narrator** only works in English and may not work well with certain software. The user is also referred to the Microsoft Web site for details of other "screen reader" software. After clicking **OK** a dialogue box appears allowing the various options to be set in Narrator.

The On-Screen Keyboard

This feature is intended for anyone with mobility problems, who finds it difficult to handle a normal keyboard. The **On-Screen Keyboard** is launched from **Start, All Programs, Accessories, Accessibility** and **On-Screen Keyboard**.

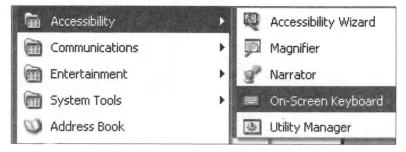

The on-screen keyboard is operated by a mouse or perhaps another type of pointing device. The cursor is moved over the required letter and the mouse is clicked, causing the letter to appear on the page at the current cursor position.

The Utility Manager

The **Utility Manager** is started from *start*, **All Programs**, **Accessories**, **Accessibility** and **Utility Manager**.

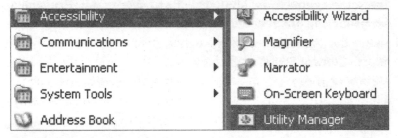

A dialogue box appears showing, within a single window, the special needs programs which are currently running. Here the programs can be started, stopped or configured.

The previous pages describe the special needs features provided free within Windows XP. The Microsoft Web site gives details of additional specialist software and hardware resources to help users with a range of impairments.

Adjusting the Screen Display

Microsoft Windows allows you to adjust the appearance of the various windows, menus and icons. You can also adjust the screen *resolution*, so that text and screen objects such as icons are displayed larger. These changes can be made using the Windows Control Panel, discussed earlier. Select **Start**, **Control Panel** and make sure the control panel is in **Category View**. (It should be displaying **Switch to Classic View** as shown below).If necessary click **Switch to Category View** on the left-hand side of the Control Panel.

Now click **Appearance and Themes,** as shown above. A list of four tasks appears, as shown on the right. If you click **Change the computer's theme,** you can choose from a drop-down menu of several colour schemes for the various windows and screen objects.

Click **Apply** and **OK** for the new settings to take effect.

The desktop background and screen saver can be changed in a similar way. The screen saver is a constantly changing display used to protect the screen when the computer is switched on but not being used.

Change the screen resolution shown on the previous page allows you to increase or decrease the size of the text and icons, etc., displayed on the screen. The resolution is the number of small squares (known as *pixels* or *picture elements*) used to map out the screen. Typical screen resolutions are 800x600, 1024x768, and 1600x 1200. Drag the sliding pointer on the scale under **Screen resolution**, to make the adjustment, then click **Apply** and **OK**.

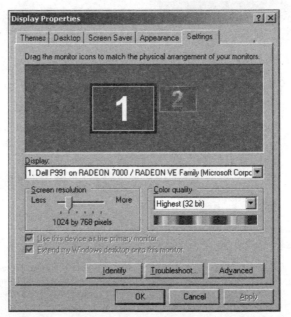

5

Getting Started with Word and Works

Introduction

Even though the examples in this book are based on one particular program, Microsoft Word, you can follow the work with any of the popular word processing programs. This is possible because most other brands of word processor, such as Corel WordPerfect and Lotus WordPro, also operate within the Microsoft Windows environment and have a similar "look and feel". These various word processing programs use similar menus and icons for tasks such as saving and printing your work; once you've mastered one program the others are easier to learn.

Two of the most popular word processing programs used throughout the world and frequently referred to in this book are Microsoft Word and the Microsoft Works Word Processor, briefly outlined below.

Microsoft Word

This is the world's leading business and professional word processing program; it can be bought separately or as part of the Microsoft Office XP integrated software package.

The Microsoft Works Word Processor

This word processor is part of the very popular Works integrated package. It is very similar to Microsoft Word. A slightly more expensive version of Works, known as Works Suite, includes Microsoft Word itself.

Installing the Software

If you don't have Microsoft Word or Works installed on your computer it's a simple matter to install it yourself. If you also want to keep records and possibly manage your accounts, etc., using a spreadsheet program, for example, then you need to buy an integrated package such as Microsoft Office XP or Microsoft Works or Works Suite. To run the latest versions of these programs you do need to have a fairly modern machine (bought in the last few years), preferably running the Windows XP operating system discussed earlier.

It only takes a few minutes to install the software; you just place the CD in its drive and sit back. The CD will "autoboot", i.e. start up on its own, and from then on you simply follow the instructions on the screen. The installation process copies the important program files onto your hard disc and may also place the name of the program on the main Windows **Start** menu as shown on the right.

The installation process will enter the name of the new program on the **All Programs** menu, as shown on the right for Microsoft Works. A similar entry on the **All Programs** menu is created when Word is installed.

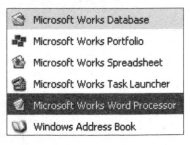

Icons for the new program may be automatically placed on the Windows Desktop during the installation process – if not they can always be put on using the method described on page 69. Shown below are desktop icons for both **Microsoft Word** and the **Microsoft Works Word Processor**.

After you have installed the word processor software, each time you use the program it will be run from the hard disc. The CD is not needed to run the program and can be stored away in a safe place. However, the CD might be needed again at some time in the future if you ever need to re-install the software after a technical problem. Or you may wish to install additional features provided on the CD which were not included in your original installation. (Some features are optional and their installation can be postponed until you find you need to use them).

Starting the Word Processor

Once installed on the hard disc, there are several ways to launch the program ready for a word processing session:

- Click the program's name on the **Start** menu
- Click the program's name on the **All Programs** menu
- Double-click the program's icon on the Windows Desktop.

The Word Processor Screen

When you launch the word processor using one of the methods just described, a blank white screen with a flashing cursor appears, ready for you to start typing. Across the top of the screen are the menu bar and the various toolbars, which are discussed in detail later.

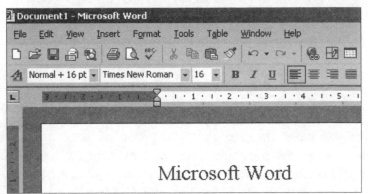

You can see from the above that both the Word and Works word processors are basically very similar. The remainder of this book will be mainly based on Word, but this should present no problems for users of the Works word processor.

Using the Keyboard

Most keyboards still follow the QWERTY convention, which refers to the order of the first six letter keys.

Some Important Keys

Capital letters are obtained by simultaneously holding the **Shift** key, shown left and below, marked with an upward pointing arrow. Or you can switch the **Caps Lock** key on and off as required.

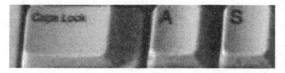

Where there are two characters on a key, the upper character is obtained by holding down the **Shift** key while the required key is pressed.

The screenshot below shows another set of important keys on the right of the keyboard.

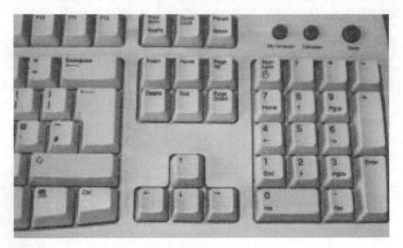

The cluster of numeric keys on the right above is the *numeric key pad*. This is often used when a large amount of numeric data is to be entered continuously.

The four keys marked with arrows, shown above, are the *cursor control keys*. These can be used to move the cursor about the screen or to step through the options on a menu. Along the top of the keyboard are the *function keys*, marked **F1** to **F12**. These can be programmed to carry out various functions. For example, **F1** is often programmed to provide help within a piece of software.

The **Backspace** key shown above is used to delete text to the left of the current cursor position. The **Delete** key removes text to the right of the current cursor position.

Also shown are duplicates of the **Shift** and **Ctrl** keys, which are also present on the left of the keyboard.

The **Enter** key shown left and on the numeric keypad on the previous page, is used to start a new line when typing. It is also known as the **Return** key, after the term Carriage Return on ordinary typewriters.

The **Insert** key shown left allows you to switch between **Insert** and **Overtype** mode. In **Insert** mode, any letters you type in the middle of a sentence push out the existing letters. In **Overtype** mode the existing letters disappear as you type over them.

The **Home** key moves the cursor to the beginning of a *line of text*. The **End** key moves the cursor to the end of a *line*.

Ctrl+Home and **Ctrl+End** move the cursor to the beginning and end of a *document*.

Page Up and **Page Down** enable you to scroll through a document approximately one *screen* at a time.

Ctrl+Page Up and **Ctrl+Page Down** enable you to scroll through a document a *page* at a time.

At the bottom of the keyboard, the long key (shown below) is the **Space Bar**, used to insert spaces between words.

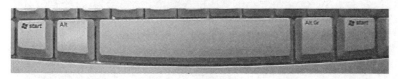

Also shown above and below is the **Windows** key, which brings up the Microsoft Windows **Start** menu.

If you don't possess typing skills you may wish to practise with one of the many typing tutor programs available such as Mavis Beacon Teaches Typing. If you learn to type properly, apart from saving time, this will allow you to concentrate on the content of your work, rather than constantly looking for keys on the keyboard.

Keyboard Shortcuts

Many people are happy to operate the computer using a mouse, by pointing and clicking over screen icons and menus. However, some people, such as trained typists, may prefer to use the keyboard instead of the mouse.

As an alternative to using the mouse, many operations can be carried out using special combinations of key presses, known as *keyboard shortcuts*. For example, to turn bold text *on* you would press the key marked **Ctrl** together with the key for the letter **B**. To turn bold text *off* you would again press **Ctrl+B**.

In general, if an effect is turned on by a keyboard shortcut, it is turned off by the same method. Keyboard shortcuts are discussed later in this chapter.

Microsoft Keyboards

Special Microsoft Windows keyboards are available which contain, amongst other things, small round buttons for connecting directly to the Internet and searching for particular Web pages. Special buttons also give direct access to Windows features such as a **Calculator** and **My Computer**, which displays information about your discs and files.

An *on-screen keyboard* is provided in Windows XP to help anyone with restricted movement. The virtual keyboard is displayed on the screen as shown below. The mouse is then used to select the required key on the screen. Clicking a letter or number causes that character to appear in the document on the screen at the current cursor position.

Tips for Healthy Typing

- Get an adjustable chair so that you can sit at the correct height with forearms and upper legs parallel to the floor. Knees and elbows should form an angle of 90 degrees. Back and thighs should also be at 90 degrees. Forearms and hands should be in line.

- The chair should have 5 legs for stability and castors for ease of movement. A good back rest is necessary to keep the back vertical and supported. A thick pad is desirable for comfort.

- Avoid clutter and obstructions reducing leg-room.

- Feet should be flat on the floor – get a foot rest if necessary.

- The head should be kept up to help blood flow.

- Position the monitor so that there is no reflected glare from lights, windows, etc. Obtain an anti-glare screen if necessary. The top of the monitor should be just below eye level.

- Make sure the mouse, keyboard, etc., are within easy reach, without stretching. To avoid straining or twisting to read a document, use a document holder with the paper at the same height as the monitor.

- Take regular breaks, e.g. every hour. Do exercises to reduce tension in the neck and shoulders.

- Look away from the screen regularly and focus on different objects to avoid eyestrain.

- To reduce fatigue use only a light touch on the keyboard and do not grip the mouse tightly.

Starting a New Document

For many people, keeping in touch with family and friends with a well thought out letter is preferable to a hastily drafted e-mail. If you are a setting up a new venture, a well-presented business plan and correspondence is essential if you are to have a professional image.

The next few pages go through the main steps in using the word processor to produce a simple document such as a letter. Initially it is suggested that you read through the text to get a feel for the skills involved. Then you may wish to practise the skills by creating a letter of your own.

Microsoft Word can be started by double-clicking its icon on the Windows Desktop or by selecting Microsoft Word from the **Start** menu or the **All Programs** menu, as discussed earlier in this chapter.

You are presented with a blank screen ready to start typing at the current cursor position, indicated by a small flashing black line as shown below.

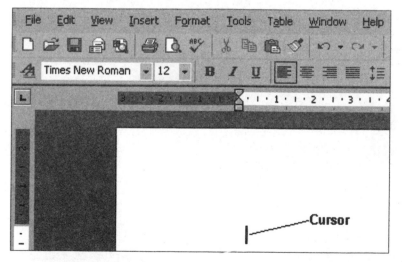

Default Settings

A word processor starts up with numerous pre-set or *default settings*, such as the size of the page margins, for example. You can safely accept many of the default values provided by the program; however, the next few pages describe some of the settings which you may prefer to change before you start entering the text of a document.

Selecting a Font

The default lettering style or *font* (often **Times New Roman**, size **12** as shown below) can easily be changed after clicking the down arrows shown right and on the toolbar below.

A drop-down menu appears as shown below, from which the required font can be selected, e.g. the popular **Arial** font.

A similar drop-down menu allows the font size to be selected from a range of sizes, measured in units of *points* ranging from 8 to 72 points. Selecting 72 points, for example, results in letters nearly an inch high. These might be suitable for a heading on a poster or newsletter, etc.

Setting the Paper Size

You need to ensure that the paper size in your document on the screen matches the actual paper used by your printer. Select **File**, **Page Setup...** and the **Paper** tab. From the drop-down menu choose the size of the paper you are using in your printer, typically **A4**, as shown below.

The **Margins** tab shown below allows you to change not only the top, bottom, right and left margins but also the **Orientation**. In **Portrait** the printout is viewed with the long sides of the page vertical while in the **Landscape** orientation the long sides of the paper are horizontal.

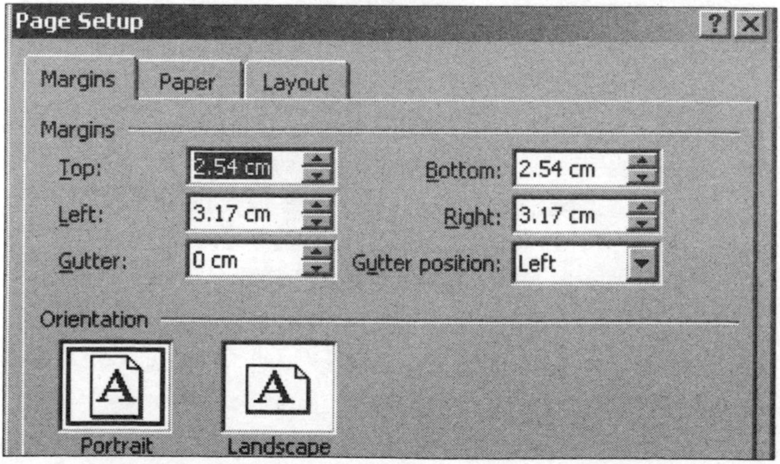

Creating a New File Using Save As...

Before entering the text of a document it's a good idea to create a file with a suitable name. Then it's a simple matter to quickly save the document at intervals while you are entering the text. Select **File** and **Save As...** and enter a meaningful **File name:** such as **Holiday in Tuscany**, for example.

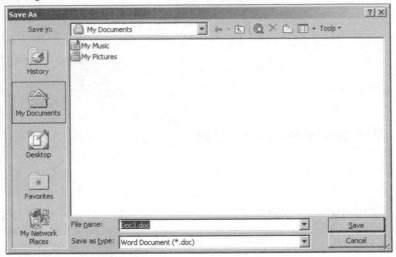

Saving Your Work

A new file will automatically be saved in the **My Documents** folder shown in the **Save in:** bar above. If you don't specify your own name for the document in the **File name:** bar shown above, the file will automatically be called **Doc1**, **Doc2**, or **Doc3**, etc. Once you have saved your work the first time click the **Save** icon every few minutes to make a permanent copy of the latest version of the document on the hard disc.

Saving and organizing your work in folders you have created is discussed in more detail later in this book.

Entering the Text of a Letter

Shown below is a short sample letter. After reading through this chapter you may wish to practise entering this letter or a similar one of your own.

Swallows Barn

Millers Dale

Staffordshire

SA3 ML6

5 June 2005

The Manager

The Eden Hotel

Chianciano Terme

Tuscany

Dear Sir/Madam

A friend has recommended your hotel to me and I would like to arrange a holiday with you in May 2006, if possible.

I would be most grateful if you could send me a copy of your latest brochure, including details of your facilities for the disabled and car hire.

I understand that your town is famous for its health-giving mineral springs; I would therefore be grateful for any further information you can provide on the various spas.

Yours faithfully

Sarah Railton

Hints for Beginners:

- You don't need to press the **Enter** or **Return** key at the end of a line. Just keep typing and the word processor takes care of everything in a process known as *word wrap*.

- Hold down the **Shift** key to obtain capital or *upper case* letters.

- You only need to press **Enter** or **Return** at the end of a line if you want to start a new paragraph or insert one or more blank lines.

- Use the **Tab** key (shown on the right) to jump across to a fixed point on a line - e.g. to vertically align the left-hand edges of the lines of an address.

Tab to each line of the address

Swallows Barn
Millers Dale
Staffordshire
SA3 ML6
5 June 2005

Correcting Mistakes While Typing

While you're entering the text, correct any typing errors by deleting the mistake then typing the correct text. Words to the *left* of the cursor are deleted with the **Backspace** key (shown left), while the **Delete** key removes text to the *right* of the cursor.

Remember to click the **Save** icon on the Toolbar at regular intervals. This will place a copy of the latest version of the document on your hard disc and can save hours of work if there's a power cut, etc.

Setting Your Own Tab Stops

When you need to start several lines of text a long way from the left margin, the **Tab** key is used to make sure that successive lines all start in exactly the same place. For example, ensuring the lines of an address are vertically aligned on the left. Beginners often use the space bar to move across the screen to the point where text is to start. Unfortunately, using this method, the alignment is often lost when the document is printed on paper. Using the **Tab** key however, the cursor jumps across to exactly the same position on every line on the screen and the alignment is maintained on the printout on paper.

Document1 - Microsoft Word

File　Edit　View　Insert　Format　Tools　Table　Window　Help

Arial ··· 10

Left Tab set at 100mm

Swallows Barn
Millers Dale
Staffordshire
SA3 ML6

In the screenshot above a left **Tab** has been set at 100mm, as discussed later. (As described shortly, you can change the units to inches or centimetres if you prefer).

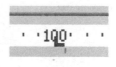

Word processors normally have several default **Tab** stops already set. However, it's useful to be able to set your own using the **Tabs** dialogue box shown below and accessed from **Format** and **Tabs**....

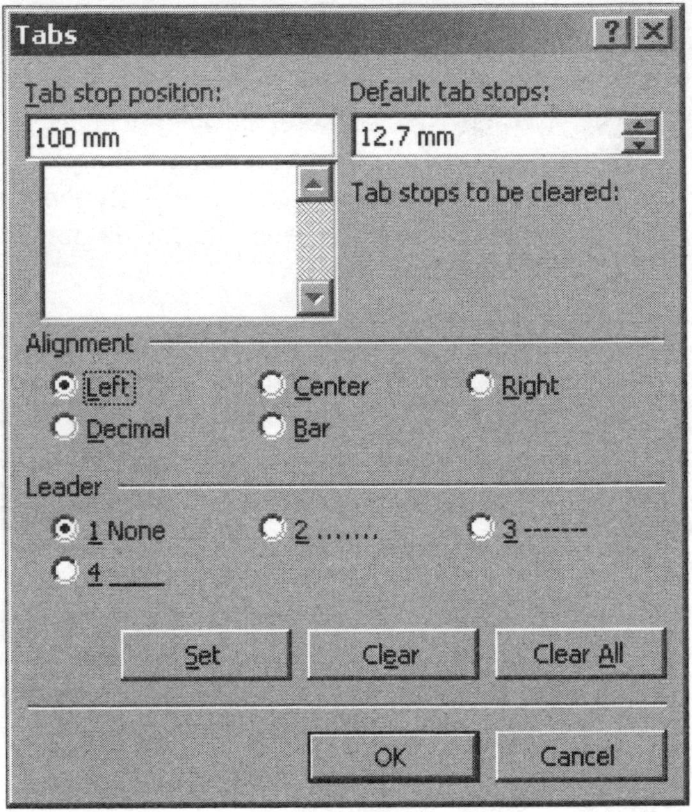

Enter the required measurement in **Tab stop position:** and click **Set** and **OK**.

If you prefer to work in inches or centimetres, select **Tools**, **Options...** and the **General** tab. Click the down arrow to the right of **Measurement units:** to change the units using the drop-down menu shown below.

Measurement units:	Millimeters ▼
☐ Show pixels for HTML	Inches
	Centimeters
	Millimeters
	Points
	Picas

E-mail Options...

OK   Cancel

Having set a **Tab** stop, press the **Tab** key to move to the required position in the document. In the **Tabs** dialogue box on the previous page, there are five different types of **Tab** stop, allowing you to align the text on the **Right, Left** or about the **Center**. The **Decimal Tab** causes columns of numbers to be vertically aligned about the decimal point. The **Bar Tab** places a vertical line at the **Tab** position.

Alignment

⦿ Left   ◯ Center   ◯ Right

◯ Decimal   ◯ Bar

You can also select the various **Tab** stops by clicking an icon on the top left of the Word screen, under the toolbars.

As you click the icon it changes, displaying in turn the various types of **Tab** stop.

Times New Roman ▼ 12 ▼

Click here to change the type of Tab stop.

When you have selected the required type of **Tab** stop as shown on the previous page, click the position on the ruler where you wish to insert the **Tab** stop, as shown below.

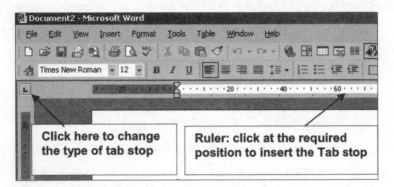

Leaders

Referring to the **Tabs** dialogue box previously, the radio buttons under the word **Leader** enable the **Tab** position to be preceded by a choice of dotted or continuous lines.

This idea is often used in the contents page of a book, for example, as shown below.

Click the required radio button, **2**, **3**, or **4** above, to include a leader up to a **Tab** stop. Leader **3** is shown in the example above.

Creating a Template for Your Own Headed Paper

To save typing in your address at the top of every letter you write, you could make a template for headed paper containing your address and any other information. Start a new document by clicking on the **New Blank Document** icon shown on the left and on the Toolbar extract below.

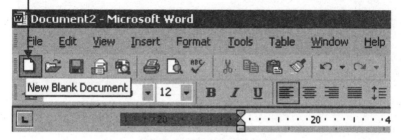

Now use the **Tab** key to set up your name and address using either the default **Tab** stops provided by Word or set up your own as previously described.

Swallows Barn
Millers Dale
Staffordshire
SA3 ML6
6 June 2005

Now click **File** and **Save As...** from the menu bar. The **Save As** dialogue box opens up as shown on the next page.

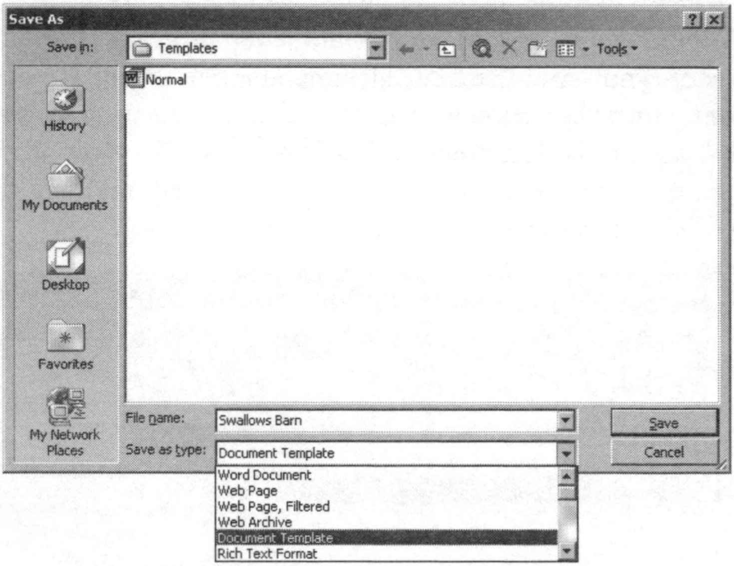

Now select **Document Template** from the drop-down menu shown above. This is obtained by clicking the down arrow at the right of the **Save as type:** bar shown above. Note that the **File name:** is automatically taken from your address, as in the **Swallows Barn** example above, but this can be changed if you wish. Also when you click **Document Template**, the **Save in:** bar above automatically changes to display the **Templates** folder as the saving destination.

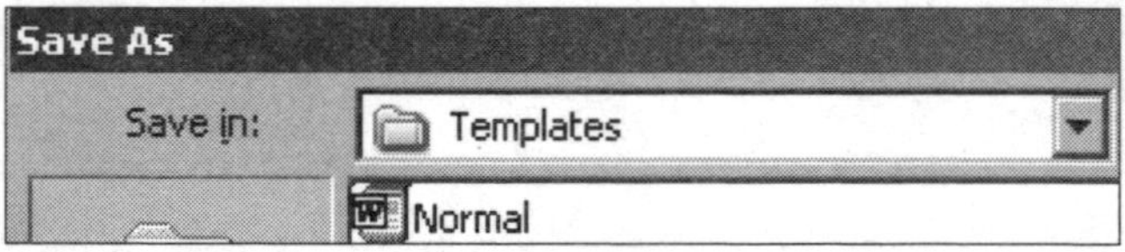

Note that the **Normal** file shown above refers to the default template provide by Word. This will automatically be used for all new documents unless you select a specific template.

When you click the **Save** button in the **Save As** dialogue box, the new template is saved alongside any existing templates in the **Templates** folder.

You can now use the new address template whenever you want to start a new letter. First select **File** and **New...** from the Menu Bar. Under **New from template**, in the **New Document** panel on the right-hand side of the

New from template

	General Templates...
	Templates on my Web Sites...
	Templates on Microsoft.com

Word screen, select **General Templates...** as shown above on the right.

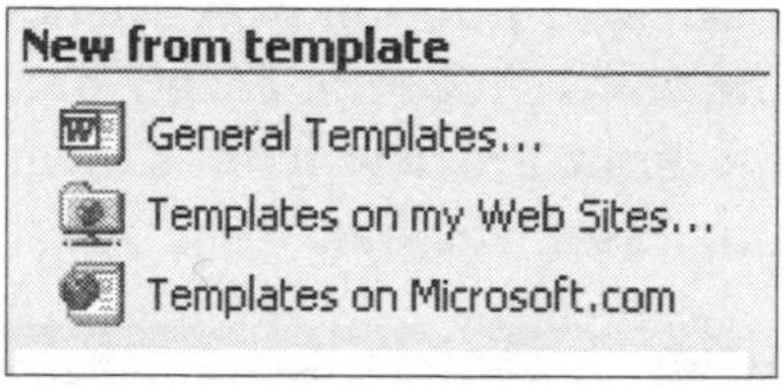

The **Templates** dialogue box opens as shown below.

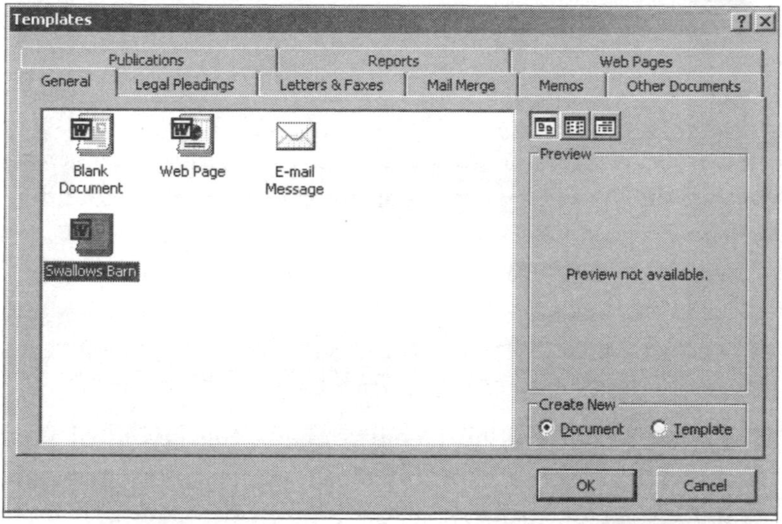

Select the new template, **Swallows Barn** in this example, and click **OK**. A new Word page opens up with the address already inserted, ready for you to start entering the text of a letter.

Printing a Letter

Print Preview

Before you make a printout on paper, you might wish to select **Print Preview** to give a screen view of how the document will print on paper. Click **File** and **Print Preview** from the word processor Menu Bar. Alternatively click the **Print Preview** icon, shown right, on the word processor Toolbar.

The **Print Preview** allows you to check the layout of your document before it is printed on paper. You may, for example, decide to insert a few blank lines here and there just to make the document more readable. When you are finished with the **Preview** click **Close** to return to the main word processor window.

Printing on Paper

Use **File** and **Print...** then click **OK** to make a copy of your letter on paper. Notice that there are options to specify the number of copies and the particular page(s) to be printed, in the case of longer documents.

Alternatively, if you just want a quick print using the existing **Print** dialogue box settings, click the **Print** icon on the word processor toolbar.

Using the **Print** icon does not allow you to alter any of the settings as shown in the **Print** dialogue box above.

Appendix 2 describes the use of the Mail Merge facility in Word to send personalized versions of a standard letter to lots of different people.

Keyboard Shortcuts

You may prefer to use the following keyboard shortcuts as an alternative to mouse operations. For example, to switch bold lettering on (and off), use **Ctrl+B**. This means "While holding down the **Ctrl** key, press the **B** key."

Ctrl+C	Copy text
Ctrl+X	Cut text
Ctrl+V	Paste text
Ctrl+Z	Undo previous action
Ctrl+A	Select entire document
Ctrl+B	Switch bold text on and off
Ctrl+U	Switch underline on and off
Ctrl+I	Switch Italic text on and off
Ctrl+E	Centre paragraph
Ctrl+J	Justify paragraph
Ctrl+L	Align paragraph left
Ctrl+R	Align paragraph right
Ctrl+Q	Remove paragraph formatting
Ctrl+1	Single-spaced text
Ctrl+5	1½ spaced text
Ctrl+2	Double-spaced text
Ctrl+N	Open new (blank) document
Ctrl+O	Open existing document
Ctrl+S	Save document
Ctrl+P	Print document

In general, the above keyboard shortcuts are applied after first selecting the block of text. As described earlier, text is selected with the mouse or by holding down the shift key and traversing the text with one of the arrow keys. Effects such as **Bold**, *Italic* and <u>Underline</u> can be switched on before the text is typed.

6
Editing and Formatting

Introduction

Once you've saved a document on your hard disc, you can retrieve it for editing at a later date. Just load the document into the computer's memory using **File** and **Open...** and it's displayed on the screen. Now you can make any changes you like – there's no need to type the whole document again. You might wish to change the date or alter a few names and addresses. Or you might want to make bigger changes such as moving, inserting or deleting paragraphs. When you've finished editing you simply save and print out the revised version including the changes.

The term "cutting and pasting" is still used to describe moving a piece of text within a document or between documents. This is done using the cutting, copying and pasting icons from the word processor toolbar as shown on the right and below.

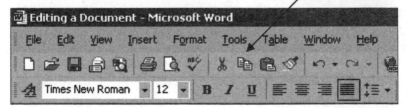

This topic is described in more detail later in this chapter and in Appendix 1.

Retrieving a Document from the Hard Disc

Having created a document and saved it on disc you can
retrieve it at any time. From the menu bar select **File** and
Open.... As discussed in the previous chapter, a letter was
saved with the name **Holiday in Tuscany**. It was saved in the
folder **My Documents**. You may need to click the down
arrow to the right of the **Look in:** bar, shown below, to
select the required folder on your **C:** drive (hard disc). If
necessary please see Chapter 10, Managing Your Word
Files, for more information on saving and organising your
work in folders.

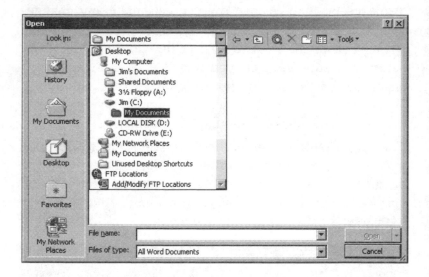

When you have located the required folder containing your
file, click on the file name so that it is highlighted, as
shown on the next page.

Now click **Open** and the document is retrieved from the hard disc and displayed on the screen in your word processor.

Now you can proof read the document on the screen and improve it using editing operations such as the following:

- Deleting text
- Replacing text
- Moving blocks of text
- Inserting words or blocks of text
- Correcting spelling mistakes
- Adding text to extend the document.

Undoing Actions

When editing a document it's easy to make a mistake like deleting the wrong words. Fortunately the **Undo** feature accessed off the **Edit** menu shown below allows you to reverse *the last action*. Or you can use the **Undo** icon off the word processor toolbar, shown right and below.

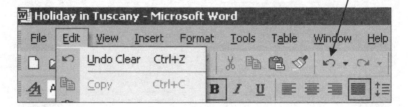

Please note that the **Undo** feature can be used to reverse a variety of editing tasks, not just deleting text as in this example. If you prefer, you can undo an action using the keyboard alternative **Ctrl+Z**, which literally means "Hold down the **Ctrl** key and press **Z**".

Block Operations on Selected Text

To delete or move entire lines, paragraphs or larger blocks
of text, first *select* the required text, so that it's *highlighted*
against a black background, as shown below.

The Spa Towns of Italy

It is traditional for many older people in Italy to spend
their holidays at one of the famous spa towns. Here you
can combine a holiday with treatment for a range of
illnesses from arthritis, liver conditions to lung and
breathing difficulties.

The spa towns often include the word Terme in their
name, signifying that they are built close to natural hot
springs with health-giving powers.

Castrocaro Terme and Chianciano Terme in Tuscany
are two well-known spa towns. Some spas have an
indoor pool and comprehensive medical facilities as
well as a restaurant while others are simply outdoor hot

Selecting Text Using the Mouse

- To select any piece of text, keep the left mouse
  button held down while moving the pointer
  across the whole of the required text.

- To select an individual word, double-click over
  the word.

- To select a line of text, make a single click in
  the left margin of the document.

- To select a paragraph, double-click in the left
  margin.

- To select the whole document, treble-click in
  the left margin or use **Edit** and **Select All** off the
  menus.

Selecting Text Using the Keyboard

In general, many of the menu options have a keyboard alternative as shown on the right. So, for example, you can select the whole document using **Ctrl+A**, as shown below on the right next to **Select All**. This means, while holding down the **Ctrl** (**Control**) key, press the letter **A**.

Edit	View	Insert	Format
⤺	Undo Clear		Ctrl+Z
↻	Repeat Clear		Ctrl+Y
✂	Cut		Ctrl+X
🗐	Copy		Ctrl+C
📋	Office Clipboard...		
📋	Paste		Ctrl+V
	Paste Special...		
	Clear		▶
	Select All		Ctrl+A

Using the Cursor Keys

Another method of selecting text is to place the cursor at the beginning of the required block of text then, while holding down the **Shift** key, shown on the right, use the cursor or arrow keys, shown below, to move over the required text. The block of text should be highlighted, i.e. selected, as shown on the previous page.

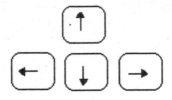

Deleting a Block of Text

Highlight the required text and press the **Delete** key. (Small pieces of text can be deleted by placing the cursor on the left of the required text and holding down the **Delete** key.)

Inserting Text

Insert text by placing the cursor where the new text is to begin then start typing. The new text should force its way in without deleting any of the old text. If the new text *over-types* and replaces the existing text rather than pushing its way in, press the **Insert** key to switch off over-type mode.

| Insert |

Find and Replace

This facility allows you to replace a word or group of words wherever they occur in a document. For example, you might wish to replace the word "house" with an alternative word such as "property". Select **Edit** and **Replace...** to open up the **Find and Replace** dialogue box.

Enter the old word in **Find what:** and enter the new word or words in **Replace with:** as shown in the next dialogue box. Now click **Replace** or **Replace All** to replace the old word(s) with the new word (s) throughout the document.

Moving a Block of Text - Cut and Paste

Sometimes you may decide that a document will read better if the order of the paragraphs is changed; traditionally this meant cutting and pasting the paper document with scissors and glue. The word processor makes this operation very much easier.

First select the block of text to be moved as shown below.

The Spa Towns of Italy

It is traditional for many older people in Italy to spend their holidays at one of the famous spa towns. Here you can combine a holiday with treatment for a range of illnesses from arthritis, liver conditions to lung and breathing difficulties.

The spa towns often include the word Terme in their name, signifying that they are built close to natural hot springs with health-giving powers.

Castrocaro Terme and Chianciano Terme in Tuscany are two well-known spa towns. Some spas have an indoor pool and comprehensive medical facilities as well as a restaurant while others are simply outdoor hot springs.

Now click the scissors icon on the toolbar, as shown on the right. This removes the selected text and stores it on the "clipboard". The clipboard is a temporary storage location where text (and graphics) can be held until you are ready to place them somewhere else in the document.

Next move the cursor to wherever you want the selected text to start. Now click the paste icon on the toolbar (shown right) to place the text in its new position, as shown below.

The Spa Towns of Italy

It is traditional for many older people in Italy to spend their holidays at one of the famous spa towns. Here you can combine a holiday with treatment for a range of illnesses from arthritis, liver conditions to lung and breathing difficulties.

Paragraph moved from here

Castrocaro Terme and Chianciano Terme in Tuscany are two well-known spa towns. Some spas have an indoor pool and comprehensive medical facilities as well as a restaurant while others are simply outdoor hot springs.

The spa towns often include the word Terme in their name, signifying that they are built close to natural hot springs with health-giving powers.

If you prefer, cutting and pasting a piece of selected text can also be achieved using the options on the **Edit** menu, either by selecting with the mouse or by using the keyboard alternatives **Ctrl+X**, **Ctrl+C** and **Ctrl+V**, as shown below.

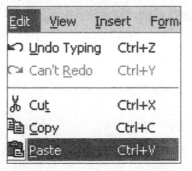

Copying a Piece of Text

If you want to *duplicate* a piece of highlighted text rather than *move* it, then use the copy icon off the menu bar shown right or the **Copy** command off the **Edit** menu shown on the previous page. Then use the paste icon **Edit** menu option to place the copied text at the position where you have placed the cursor.

Using the clipboard for moving and copying is a useful skill in a variety of Windows applications, not just for moving text within a document. Cutting, copying and pasting using the clipboard are discussed in more detail in Appendix 1.

Checking Spelling

The spelling checker invoked from **Tools** and **Spelling and Grammar...** suggests alternative spellings, improvements in grammar and spacing between words.

Spelling and Grammar: English (U.K.)	? X
Not in Dictionary:	
Here you can combine a holiday with treatment for a range of illnesses from arthritus, liver conditions to lung and breathing difficulties.	Ignore Once / Ignore All / Add to Dictionary
Suggestions:	
arthritis	Change / Change All / AutoCorrect
Dictionary language: English (U.K.)	
☑ Check grammar	Options... / Undo / Close

Formatting a Document

After you have checked the content and spelling in a document, you may want to change the appearance. This is known as *formatting* and includes different fonts or styles and sizes of lettering and text effects such as bold, italics and underlining. Formatting also includes page layout features such as the margins between the text and the edges of the page, alterations to the space between lines of text and various ways of aligning the vertical edges of the text.

If you know the formatting you want to use, it can be set before you begin typing. For example, you could switch italics on before typing a particular word then switch it off after the word. Alternatively, you can enter the text of your document without any effects and then apply the formatting afterwards.

The Formatting Toolbar

On the left of the toolbar extract shown above is the font name and size, changed by clicking the down arrows and selecting from the drop-down menus.

Next are the three main text effects bold, italic and underline. These effects can also 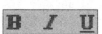 be switched on by holding down the **Ctrl** key and pressing either **B**, **I** or **U**. Effects like these operate as "toggles" – you use the same method to switch them on as to switch them off.

Moving along to the right the formatting toolbar, 4 icons represent different methods of text alignment.

Reading from left to right, the actions of the 4 icons on the right and their alternative keyboard shortcuts are:

- Aligned left edge, ragged right   **Ctrl+L**

- Aligned to the centre   **Ctrl+E**

- Aligned right, ragged left   **Ctrl+R**

- Justified text (aligned left and right)   **Ctrl+J**

- Remove any of the above.   **Ctrl+Q**

The problem with fully justified text is that in order to achieve the vertical alignment on the right-hand edge, the text may be filled with too many spaces between words producing unsightly "rivers of white".

The two icons towards the right of the formatting toolbar above allow lists to be highlighted with either numbers or bullets.

The next two formatting tools shown on the right are used to decrease or increase the indent at the start of a paragraph.

Applying Formatting Effects:

1 Select (or highlight) the required block of text.

2 Apply the formatting by clicking the appropriate icon on the toolbar, or selecting the relevant menu command or using the equivalent keyboard shortcut.

3 When the formatting has taken effect, remove the highlighting by clicking outside of the selected area.

Changing Line Spacing

Sometimes you may want to set a paragraph or indeed a whole document with extra spacing between lines. Double spacing, for example, is often used on draft documents to allow extra space for comments and suggestions to be added by hand. Highlight the text to be altered then select **Format** and **Paragraph...** from the Menu Bar. Line spacing can be adjusted after clicking the **Indents and Spacing** tab.

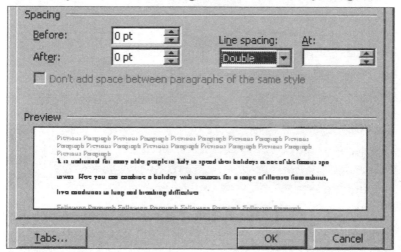

Spacing Before: and **After:** shown above allows you to insert a precise mount of extra space (in units of points, for example) before and after a paragraph.

Changing the Page Margins

The margins are the spaces between the text and the edge of the paper. The top and bottom margins are set by default at 25.4mm (or 1 inch) while the left and right margins are set at 31.7mm. (Please see the notes on page 101 if you prefer to work in other units such as inches or centimetres). You might want to increase the size of the margins to allow comments to be written on a draft document or decrease them to allow more text to fit on a page. To change the margins select **File, Page Setup...** and the **Margins** tab.

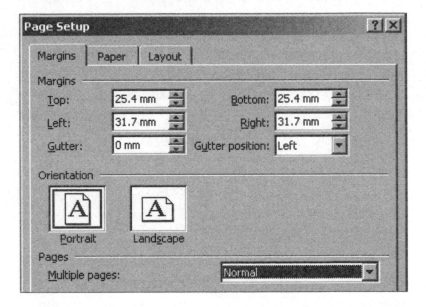

The **Gutter:** margin listed above refers to space along the left or top side of a page. This might be needed if the document is to be bound, to prevent the text being obscured by the binding.

Introducing Desktop Publishing

Introduction

The first word processors were only used for processing plain text and were a development of the electronic typewriter. They were not capable of the effects we now call desktop publishing, i.e. letters in various styles or fonts, borders and shading in different patterns and colours and everything needed to make the most elaborate poster, flyer or advertisement, etc. In the early days of computing it was usual to type the plain text of a document in a word processor, then transfer the file to a separate program dedicated to desktop publishing.

Nowadays, the ordinary user can probably find all of the desktop publishing features they need in word processing programs like Microsoft Word. However, specialist DTP programs are still used by publishing professionals and the most popular software includes Adobe PageMaker, Adobe InDesign, QuarkXpress and Corel VENTURA. For the home and small business user there are cheaper DTP packages such as Serif Page Plus and Microsoft Publisher.

However, as the following chapters attempt to show, Microsoft Word has a great deal of DTP capability which should enable you to produce a wide variety of documents such as newsletters, magazines, leaflets, flyers, invitations business cards and complete books.

The desktop publishing features covered in this chapter are:

- Fonts or different styles and sizes of lettering
- Pages of text divided into two or more columns
- Inserting a picture or photograph into a page of text and adjusting its size and position
- Selecting clip art from an online library and inserting it into a Word document
- Capturing screenshots including Web pages and Web pictures and inserting into a Word document.

Working with Fonts

A font is a style of lettering in a particular size. You can see the different fonts installed on your computer by clicking the arrow to the right of the current font name, shown below.

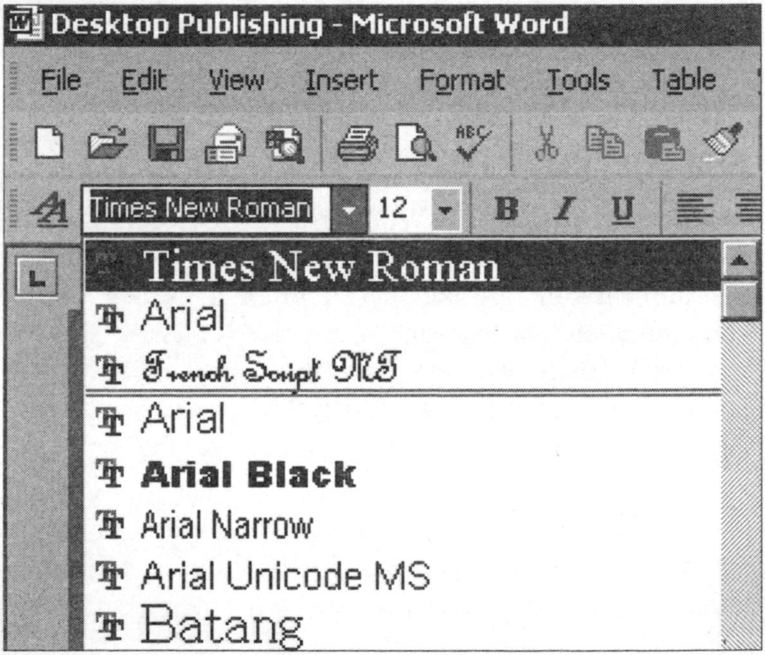

You will probably find there are far more fonts than you can ever use. Many beginners, when first seeing the huge variety of fonts available, produce documents using an excess of different fonts. It's a good idea to look at a few professional documents – you'll often find that in more formal documents no more than two fonts, such as **Times New Roman** and **Arial** have been used. Even with only two fonts, you can still emphasise words using features such as bold, italics, underlining and capital letters.

Of course in more light-hearted material such as invitations or greetings cards, etc., you can get away with the more exotic fonts such as *Vivaldi* or *Blackadder ITC*.

The text size is selected from the drop-down menu to the right of the current font size, **12** in this example.

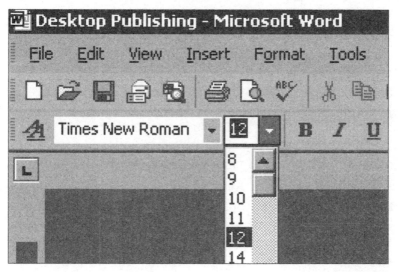

If you can't see the font size you want in the drop-down menu, try typing it manually into the slot at the top, as shown on the right.

This book is mainly set in the Times New Roman font at size 12. The commonly used unit for font size in the printing world is the *point*; there are 72 points to the inch. The example below is set at 36 points or half an inch.

Times New Roman

Applying a Font

- You can select the font name and size as previously described, before you begin typing.
- You can take an existing document and change the fonts throughout the whole document or just in selected parts of it.

Changing Fonts in an Existing Document

Highlight the text to be changed as shown below then select the new font and font size as described on the previous page.

> *This is done by highlighting the text as required then selecting the new font and font size.*

When you are happy with the new font and size, click outside of the selected area to remove the highlighting.

Even more control of fonts is given by the **Font** dialogue box, shown on the next page and opened using **Format** and **Font...** from the Word Menu Bar. Apart from selecting the font and font size as discussed earlier, you can specify bold and italic, the **Font Color** and various **Effects** such as the **Outline** font shown on the next page.

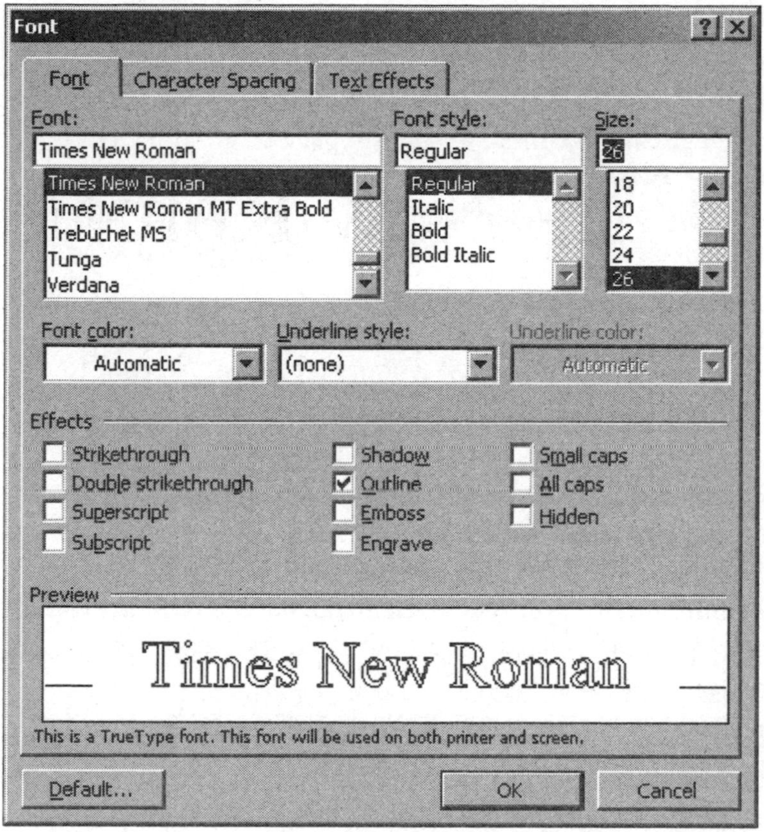

To switch on one of the **Effects**, use the mouse to tick the box at the side of the effect, as shown above next to **Outline**. Then click **OK** to apply the effect as shown below.

Outline Effect

The **Subscript** effect shown above might be used in chemistry, for example, to refer to a chemical formula such as O_2. **Superscript** might be used to refer the reader to a footnote, as in **The Sistine Chapel**[3], for example.

Using Text in Columns and Inserting Pictures

This section discusses the leaflet on Venice shown on the next page. This format might also be useful for a newsletter or magazine. I arrived at this simple design after looking at one or two commercially produced documents. Only two fonts have been used although the sub-headings have been emphasized by the use of bold, italics and capital letters.

Although a two-column format has been chosen, it's just as easy to use three columns, as employed by some magazines. The setting of columns is discussed shortly.

The three Venice photographs were "downloaded" from my digital camera and saved on the hard disc. To reproduce photographic *prints* in a Word document, they will need to be *scanned* and saved on the hard disc. If you are not familiar with handling photos from a digital camera or scanning existing prints, more details are given in my book:

"Digital Photography and Computing for the Older Generation" from Bernard Babani (publishing) Ltd.

Before starting work you need to have your pictures ready in a known location on your hard disc. My photographs were stored in the folder **C:\Venice 2005**, as shown below.

Venice

ST.MARK'S SQUARE
There is so much to see in Venice that you may need more than one visit to take in the major sights. A good place to start is St. Mark's Square. The square was originally just a space in front of the Basilica of St. Mark, the private chapel of the Doge or head of the Venetian state.

As well as the magnificent architecture of the Basilica, there are shops and open air cafés around the square. The Basilica was originally dedicated to St. Mark in 832 but was destroyed by fire in an uprising in 976. The ruined buildings were restored and consecrated in 1094. Next to St. Mark's Basilica is the Ducal or Doge's Palace, started in the 9th century and built for the Doge and the justices of Venice.

THE BRIDGE OF SIGHS
This connects the Doge's palace to the Prisons and derives its name from the reaction of the prisoners on their way to begin their sentences.

THE GRAND CANAL
Perhaps the greatest wonder of Venice is its location in the lagoon off the mainland of Italy. The Grand Canal through the middle of Venice and the network of smaller canals around it are the main route by which most visitors arrive and all supplies are delivered to the city. As there are no cars or lorries this makes walking around the city a great pleasure.
Of course, no visit to Venice would be complete without a ride on the canals in one of the many famous Gondolas.

Setting the Margins and Paper Size

First a new blank page was selected using the **New Blank Document** icon on the Word Toolbar, shown right. The **Paper size** was set at **A4** using **File** and **Page Setup...** as previously discussed. **Page Setup** was also used to set the top and bottom margins each at **25 mm** and the left and right margins each at **15 mm**.

Entering the Heading

The font for the heading **Venice** was set at **Georgia 36** point with bold, italic and centred text switched on.

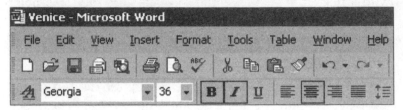

Specifying Text in Two Columns

After typing the heading **Venice** it was necessary to set the remainder of the page in two columns. To do this, place the cursor on the first line where you want the two column layout to start. Now select **Format** and **Columns...** from the Word Menu Bar. The **Columns** dialogue box opens as shown below:

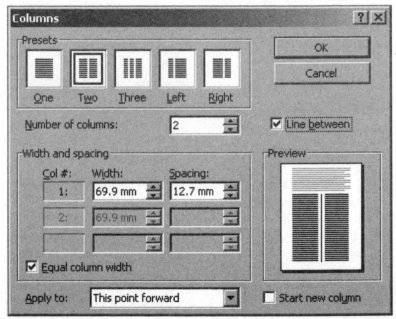

As shown in the **Columns** dialogue box on the previous page, the number of columns has been set (under **Presets**) to **Two**. A **Line between** the columns has been specified with a tick. It is also essential to make sure that **This point forward** has been selected in the **Apply to** bar at the bottom of the **Columns** dialogue box.

Entering the Text in the Columns

Next the body text was entered, starting at the top of the left-hand column. In this example, the body text has been set at **Times New Roman** size **14** point as shown below. Fully justified text is switched on by clicking the icon shown on the right.

The sub-headings can be formatted by switching on bold and italics before typing and using the **Shift** key shown right or the **Caps Lock** key to get capital letters. Or you can apply these effects after typing the text by highlighting the sub-heading and selecting bold and italic. Capital letters can be obtained by highlighting the sub-heading and selecting **Format** and **Change Case**....

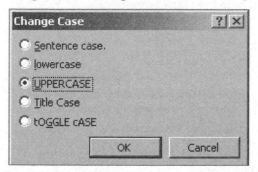

Make sure the correct **Case** option is selected and click **OK**.

Working with Pictures

Pictures can be inserted at the appropriate place in a Word document as the text is entered. Alternatively, you can insert pictures after all of the text has been entered. As stated earlier, you need to know the file name and the folder in which the picture is located, such as **C:\Venice 2005** shown below.

You can see in the above extract from the Windows Explorer that the files all end in the file name extension **.jpg**. This is the JPEG (Joint Photographic Experts Group) format, a popular way of storing digital photographs. If you want to switch on the display of file name extensions, in the Windows Explorer select **Tools**, **Folder Options...** and **View**. Now click to *remove* the tick in the box next to **Hide extensions for known file types** as shown below.

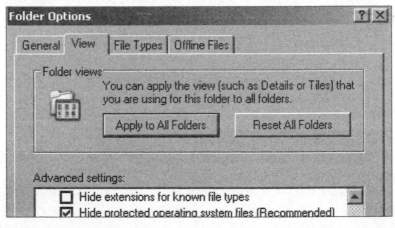

Inserting a Picture into a Word Document

Place the cursor at the position where you want the top left-hand corner of the picture to appear, as shown on the lower left below.

Now we need to retrieve a copy of the required photograph from the hard disc. This is done using **Insert**, **Picture** and **From File...** from the Word Menu Bar. Next select the folder containing the pictures, from the **Look in** bar shown below. In this example the required folder is **Venice 2005**.

In this example, **basilica.jpg** has been selected and is shown highlighted in the previous screenshot. Now click the **Insert** button shown on the previous page. The picture is inserted in the Word document at the current cursor position. If you click anywhere over the picture you will see that it is immediately surrounded by eight small black rectangles.

Formatting a Picture

The eight rectangles allow the picture to be resized and moved by dragging. However, you can obtain far greater control and precision by *formatting* the picture first. To do this first click over the picture so that the solid black rectangles appear. Then select **Format** and **Picture** off the Word Menu Bar and click the **Layout** tab as shown on the next page.

There are various ways to wrap the text around the picture, such as the **Square** and **Tight** styles as shown above. When you've set the **Wrapping style** and **Horizontal alignment** click **OK** and the small squares around the pictures change to eight empty circles as shown below.

You should now have precise control to *resize* the picture by dragging the empty circles with the mouse. The picture can be *moved* after allowing the cursor to hover anywhere over the picture until four arrows appear. Now, if necessary, use the mouse to drag the picture to its final position anywhere in the document.

There are several other formatting effects which can be applied to pictures. First select the picture by clicking over it so that the eight empty circles appear. Now select **Format**, **Picture** and **Colors and Lines**. This will allow you to put a frame around the picture with a choice of **Line Color**, **Style** and **Weight** i.e. thickness.

Line			
Color:	▓▓▓▓▓ ▼	Style:	══════ ▼
Dashed:	▬▬▬ ▼	Weight:	7.75 pt ▲▼

If you intend to print your pictures in colour, then make sure the **Color** is set to **Automatic** in the **Picture** tab of the **Format Picture** dialogue box shown in the extract below. For these particular books, as there is no colour used, **Color** is set at **Grayscale**.

Image control			
Color:	Automatic ▼		
Brightness:	◄ ▨▨ □ ▨▨ ►	50 %	▲▼
Contrast:	◄ ▨▨ □ ▨▨ ►	50 %	▲▼

You can also adjust the **Brightness** and **Contrast** in a selected picture by dragging the slider bars shown above.

The Picture Toolbar

When you select a picture in Word, by clicking anywhere within it, the **Picture** Toolbar shown below appears. This can also be switched on permanently by selecting **View**, **Toolbars** and **Picture** from the Word Menu Bar.

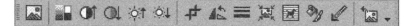

You can see the function of any of the icons on the above toolbar by allowing the cursor to hover over the icon. However, in the present context, the four icons shown on the right below are of immediate interest. These allow you to adjust the contrast and brightness of a selected picture.

Cropping

This removes actual areas around one or more of the sides of a picture in the same way as a photographic print could be cut down with scissors or guillotine. To crop a picture, select it so that the eight empty circles appear. Next select the **Crop** tool shown right from the **Picture** Toolbar shown above. Eight cropping handles appear around the picture. The picture is cropped by dragging the handles inwards as required.

Inserting Clip Art into a Word Document

Once you've got the hang of working with pictures you can move them about and resize and crop them as much as you like to get the desired result. Photographs are obviously very useful to add life to a letter to be sent to friends or family. However, if you're producing a magazine, flyer or advertisement, etc., you might want to introduce some more humorous cartoon-type material. Libraries consisting of thousands of ready-made drawings and paintings are available on the Internet and sometimes given away on free CDs. These images are collectively known as *clip art*. With so much choice, you can usually find a relevant picture, whatever the subject or event you are illustrating.

To insert clip art in Microsoft Word select **Insert**, **Picture** and **Clip Art...** from the Menu Bar. This opens up the **Insert Clip Art** Task Pane down the right-hand side of the screen. At the bottom of the Task Pane are three options including **Clips Online** shown right.

See also
🔲 Clip Organizer...
⚫ Clips Online
? Tips for Finding Clips

This is a link to a Microsoft Web site providing thousands of pictures. Clip art is often free, although it's advisable to obtain permission if you intend to reproduce an image for commercial purposes

If your computer has an Internet connection, select **Clips Online** shown above to open up the Microsoft Office Online Web site reproduced on the next page. There are lots of categories of clip art (and other media) many of which contain more than 100 pages of "clips".

FEATURED COLLECTIONS

Summer	Birthdays	Flowers	Office Supplies

Clip tips
- See larger clip art thumbnails
- Find answers to clip art questions

BROWSE CLIP ART AND MEDIA CATEGORIES

• Abstract	• Emotions	• Realistic
• Academic	• Fantasy	• Religion
• Agriculture	• Flags	• Sciences
• Animals	• Food	• Seasons
• Arts	• Government	• Signs

The small sample of clips shown below was obtained by selecting the **Flowers FEATURED COLLECTION** shown above.

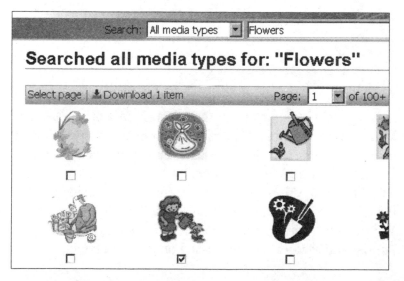

Now select one or more clips by clicking the adjacent tick box. A **Download** button on the left of the screen enables you to transfer your selected "basket" of clips from the Internet to your computer. The downloaded clip art is automatically placed in a folder called the **Microsoft Clip Organiser**, shown below.

Selection Basket

Selected items: **1**

Download size: **62 KB**

(<1 min @ 56 Kbps)

Review basket

Download 1 item ⬇

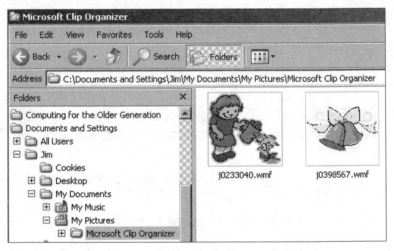

The method to insert the clip art into a word document is now exactly the same as that described earlier for the Venice photographs. The picture is inserted by clicking **Insert**, **Picture** and **From File...** and then selecting the correct folder and file. Then click the **Insert** button to place the clip art on the page at the current cursor position. Next the clip art is clicked to highlight or select the image on the Word page. Finally the picture is formatted by selecting **Format** and **Picture...** as discussed on the next page.

Wrapping Text Around a Picture

In the **Format Picture** dialogue box shown below, the **Layout** tab has been selected and the **Wrapping style** has been set at **Tight**.

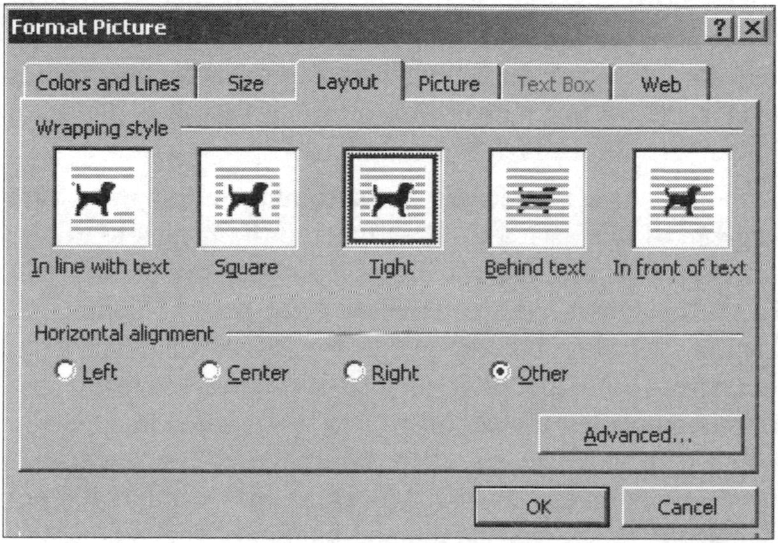

In the example below the **Advanced** button shown above was used to set the text a distance of 2mm from the picture.

Gardening

Gardening is a hobby which can be enjoyed by young and old and male and female alike. Whether you have a small window box or rolling acres you can get pleasure from this most natural of activities. Even if you live in the city, you may be able to rent an allotment and enjoy producing your own fresh fruit and vegetables. Apart from the friendships which develop amongst fellow gardeners, there are health benefits such as getting exercise and being out in the fresh air.

Inserting a Screenshot into Word

It's very useful to be able to capture a copy of your computer screen and incorporate all or part of it into a Word Document. For example, if you want to explain to a friend how to do something on the computer – after all without such a facility books like this one would be all text. Alternatively you might want to capture extracts from a Web page currently displayed on the screen and put them into an article, magazine or newsletter.

Although there is specialist art and image editing software capable of this task, you already have the means to do the job perfectly well. This is the *print screen* key on the right of the keyboard, usually labelled **Print Scrn** or something similar. Pressing this key makes a copy of whatever is on the screen and places it on the Windows clipboard. As discussed earlier, the clipboard is a store which temporarily holds text and images. After the image of the screen has been placed on the keyboard it can be inserted into a Word document at the current cursor position. This is done by clicking **Edit** and **Paste** on the Word Menu Bar or by clicking the **Paste** icon on the Toolbar.

Once inserted on the Word page the screenshot can be formatted, moved, resized and cropped just like any of the pictures, photographs and clip art discussed earlier in this chapter. Cutting, copying and pasting using the clipboard are discussed in more detail in Appendix 1.

Editing a Screen Image

Instead of pasting a screenshot straight into Word, I often paste it into the Microsoft Paint program **Start, All Programs, Accessories** and **Paint**.

This is a drawing and painting program and is provided as a component of Microsoft Windows. **Paint** has a range of tools which allow you to edit the screenshot, cutting out unwanted areas, making drawing alterations and adding annotations, etc. Then you select the area of the screenshot you require before using **Edit** and **Copy** from the Paint Menu Bar to copy the image to the clipboard. Now open up the Word document and use **Edit** and **Paste** off the Word Menu Bar to place the edited screenshot into the Word page. Alternatively click the **Paste** icon on the Word Toolbar as shown on the previous page. Cutting, copying and pasting using the clipboard are discussed in more detail in Appendix 1.

Capturing the Entire Screen

Sometimes you can't copy the whole of a screen display because essential parts of it are obscured by various toolbars, etc. This can be remedied by selecting **View** and **Full Screen** from the Word Toolbar. When you press **Print Screen**, the entire screen is captured excluding the toolbars, etc. To return to the normal screen, press the **Esc** key or click **Close Full Screen** on the small pop-up menu which appears, as shown on the right.

Capturing a Picture from a Web Page

A picture on a Web page can be saved as a separate file, instead of capturing the whole screen using the **Print Scrn** key as just discussed. Of course, before using a picture from a Web page for any *commercial* purpose you should obtain permission from the owners of the site.

Right-click over the required picture on the Web page and a menu appears, as shown above. This allows you to **Save Picture As...**, for example, a JPEG file, in a folder of your choice. Then the picture can be inserted into a Word document using **Insert**, **Picture** and **From File...**, from the Word Menu Bar, as discussed on page 133. Then, if necessary, the picture can be formatted, moved, resized and cropped, as discussed on page 134 onwards.

8

Getting Creative

Introduction

This chapter looks at some of the more spectacular desktop publishing effects available in Microsoft Word to make a document more eye-catching and interesting. These effects apply more to short documents such as flyers, leaflets, advertisements and greetings cards, etc.

The main desktop publishing effects and features described in this chapter are:

- Text boxes which can be moved around the page
- Borders and shading in different styles
- Bullets and numbers to emphasise lists
- Microsoft WordArt to manipulate and distort letters into various shapes and along curved paths
- Ready-made templates providing designs for special documents such as flyers, greetings cards, etc.

As previously stated, it's worth having a look at a few professionally produced documents for inspiration. The following leaflet is intended to advertise a charity event, but the same skills could be used to create any sort of single-page flyer, poster, or greeting card, etc. The finished leaflet is shown on the next page; subsequent pages explain the various steps needed to create the leaflet.

The poster shown above relies heavily on the use of *text boxes*. Apart from the cup and saucer sketch ("clip art" was discussed in the last chapter) and the curved lettering or WordArt (discussed shortly), the leaflet consists entirely of text boxes.

Working With Text Boxes

The text boxes in this example are the five rectangles shown below, each displaying the temporary cross-hatched border and eight empty circles which appear when a text box is selected. Entering text into text boxes has several advantages in a document of this type, compared with entering text straight onto the main Word page. Firstly, each text box can be moved around independently to adjust its position. Secondly, each text box can be *formatted* separately with its own fonts, borders and fill patterns and colours.

In the above screenshot, for the purpose of this explanation, all of the text boxes have been selected simultaneously. In practice it is usually more convenient to select and work on individual text boxes.

Selecting Text Boxes

- To select a single text box, click anywhere over the box so that eight white circles appear. The text box can now be resized or moved by dragging.

- To select several of the text boxes simultaneously, hold down the **Shift** key while clicking over each text box in turn. The text boxes now form a group and can be moved, copied or deleted as a single entity.

- To deselect a text box or group of text boxes, click anywhere outside of the box(es).

Inserting a Text Box

A text box can be inserted after selecting **Insert** and **Text Box** from the Word Menu Bar. Alternatively click the **Text Box** icon on the Drawing Toolbar, shown right and below.

If you can't see the Drawing Toolbar as shown above, click **View** and **Toolbars** from the Word Menu Bar. Then click **Drawing** from the list of toolbars. **Drawing** should now be ticked in the list and the above Drawing Toolbar should be displayed on your screen.

After clicking the **Text Box** icon, the drawing canvas appears containing the message **Create your drawing here**. I usually press **Esc** at this point to get rid of the drawing canvas and simply use the cursor (now in the shape of a cross) to drag out a text box of the required size.

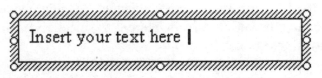

Insert your text here |

Entering Text into a Text Box

Now start entering the text into the text box. You can select the font before or after entering the text. In fact you can format existing text inside a text box in the same way as text on the main Word page. Just select the text first by dragging over it with the mouse so that the text is highlighted.

The text for the flyer heading was entered first then selected and
formatted as **Georgia 36** point **bold**.

Adding a Border to a Text Box

The text box was selected by clicking inside the box, so that the eight white circles appeared. Then **Format** and **Text Box...** were selected from the Word Menu Bar. The **Format Text Box** dialogue box appears as shown below.

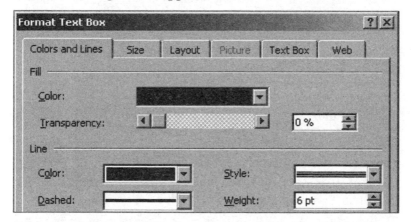

With the **Colors and Lines** tab selected as shown above, you can use the drop-down menus under **Line** next to **Color**, **Dashed, Style** and **Weight** to choose text box borders in a variety of colours, patterns and styles.

White Text Against a Black Background

The black background for the Coffee Evening text box was obtained by selecting the text box and then selecting black from the drop-down menu which appears next to **Fill** and **Color** on the **Format Text Box** dialogue box, shown below.

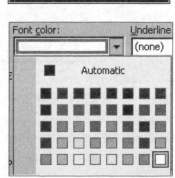

To obtain the white text in the heading **Coffee Evening**, the text box was selected then **Format** and **Font...** were selected from the Word Menu Bar. The **Font** tab was selected in the **Font** dialogue box and then white was chosen from the drop-down menu under **Font color:**.

Using Bullets and Numbers in Lists

In the middle of the flyer shown earlier, it was decided to emphasise the list of attractions by the use of bullets. These are usually solid circles or other shapes down the left-hand side against each item in a list. In this example, a more elaborate bullet has been selected as shown below

Note in the above example that the list of attractions has been split between two separate text boxes. This enables bullets to be used down the left-hand side of each list. If you simply use **Tab** (without a separate text box) to produce the right-hand list, you would not be able to use bullets.

In general, to apply bullets to a list, first enter all of the text for the list. Then select the list so that it's all highlighted. Now select **Format** and **Bullets and Numbering...** from the Word Menu Bar. The **Bullets and Numbering** dialogue box opens allowing you to select the appropriate tab as shown on the next page.

(You can, of course, use bullets and numbers to highlight a list in any type of Word document, not just in text boxes as shown in this particular example. For example, plain round bullets are used to emphasise lists in the ordinary text of this book on page 145 and 148.)

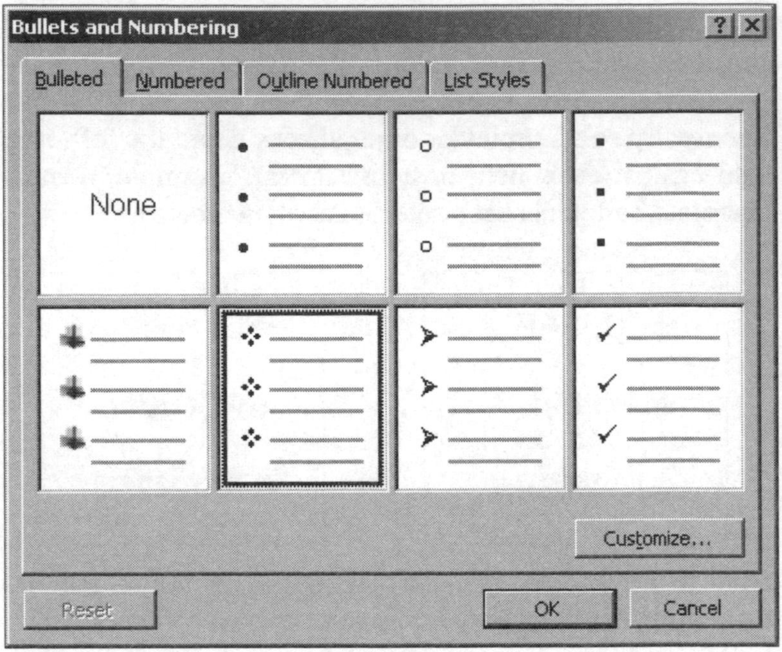

After selecting the style of bullets or numbering click **OK** to apply them. To remove bullets or numbering, highlight the list then select either the **Bulleted** tab or the **Numbered** tab. Then click **None** to remove the bullets or numbering. The **Customise...** button shown above allows you to select bullets based on a large range of special characters in different fonts and also use pictures as bullets.

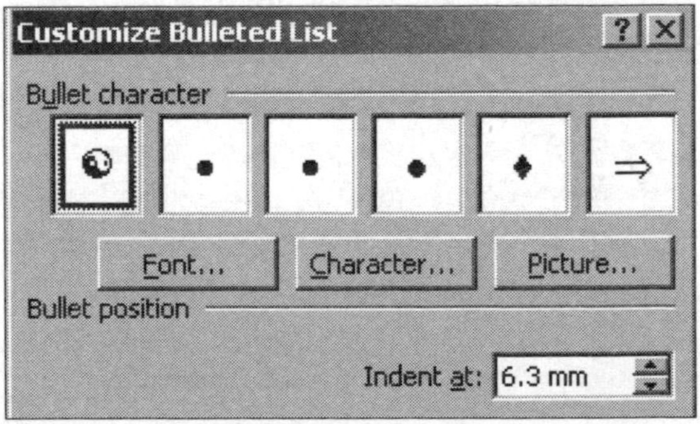

Applying a Patterned Background

In the coffee evening flyer, a pattern was used as the background to two of the text boxes. The background is applied after first selecting the text box (or to select both text boxes simultaneously hold down **Shift** while clicking each box). Now select **Format**, **Text Box...**, **Colors and Lines**. Under **Fill**, select the drop-down menu to the right of **Color** as shown on page 150. From the drop-down menu select **Fill Effects...** and then click the **Pattern** tab on the **Fill Effects** dialogue box shown below. Click the required pattern before clicking **OK** to apply the background shading to the text box(es). As shown below, there is a choice of foreground and background colours for the pattern.

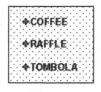

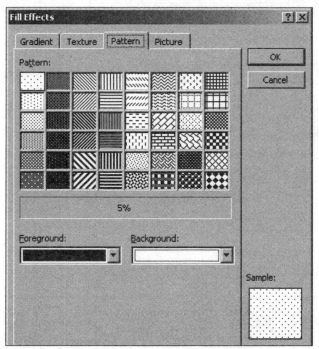

Using WordArt

As mentioned previously, WordArt is a feature in Microsoft Word which allows you to bend words into different shapes. An example is the following extract from the Coffee Evening leaflet on page 146.

To insert a piece of text in a WordArt format, click the **Insert WordArt** icon on the Drawing Toolbar, shown right and below.

Draw ▾ ⌖ AutoShapes ▾ \ ⬉ ☐ ○ ▤ ◁ ⟳ ▨ ▨

The **WordArt Gallery** opens as shown in the extract below.

When you've selected a WordArt style click **OK** and the following window appears, allowing you to enter the WordArt text.

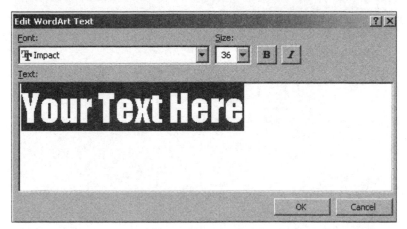

Just delete the words **Your Text Here** and replace with your own words. At this stage you can also change the font and font size using the drop-down menus launched by clicking the arrows shown above. After clicking **OK** the WordArt is inserted in the Word page at the current cursor position.

Editing WordArt

Once on the page, a piece of WordArt behaves rather like a picture. It can be formatted in the same way as a picture by setting the text wrapping and moving and resizing. If you now click over the WordArt to select it, eight small rectangles appear.

Now select **Format** and **WordArt...** from the Word Menu Bar and click the **Layout** tab shown below.

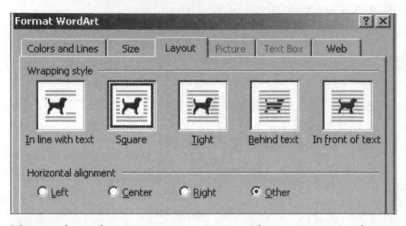

Next select the **Wrapping style**, such as **Square**, shown above. Also select the **Horizontal alignment** such as **Left**, **Center** or **Right**. After clicking **OK**, the small black squares are now replaced by empty circles as shown below.

Now the piece of WordArt can be resized or moved around the page by dragging in the same way as a picture, discussed earlier in this book.

Rotating a Piece of WordArt

The extra circle above the **W** in the above example allows a piece of WordArt to be rotated. Remember to select the WordArt first so that the circles appear as shown above.

When you select a piece of WordArt, a small toolbar appears as shown below. This toolbar enables you to modify a selected piece of WordArt.

You can find out the function of each of the icons by allowing the cursor to hover over the icon. For example, the first icon on the left allows you to insert another piece of WordArt, whereas **Edit Text...** allows you to change the words. The next icon allows you to select a different style from the **WordArt Gallery** as shown at the bottom of page 154.

WordArt can be formatted after clicking the icon shown on the right. This includes changing the colours, the text wrapping and the horizontal alignment. The icon shown on the right and on the WordArt Toolbar below allows you to select a **WordArt Shape**, complementing the **WordArt Gallery** on page 154.

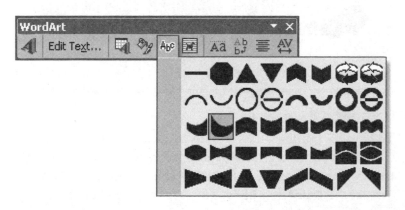

A few examples of the use of WordArt are shown below.

Creating a Page Border

The page border shown above and also on the earlier Coffee Evening leaflet was applied after selecting **Format, Borders and Shading...** and the **Page Border** tab. Then you can set the **Color** and **Style**, etc., for the page border.

Putting the Skills to Work

We have now covered all of the skills necessary to produce a document like the Coffee Evening flyer shown earlier. These skills, together with clip art mentioned in the previous chapter, can be used to produce virtually any sort of flyer, greeting card, etc. When I was a teacher I found these skills invaluable for creating posters, etc., to advertise forthcoming events and more recently for promoting a local charity event. The finished posters, etc., can be made more attractive by printing on coloured paper or thin card.

Mass Producing Tickets

If you are helping to organize an event you can use Word to produce the tickets. Simply create one ticket in a text box, then **Copy** it to the clip board and **Paste** it repeatedly onto the Word page in the form of a grid. Leave enough space for cutting up the finished cards. (To select a group of tickets for "pasting", hold down the **Shift** key and click over each ticket). Then print as many pages as you require, preferably using a stiff, coloured card.

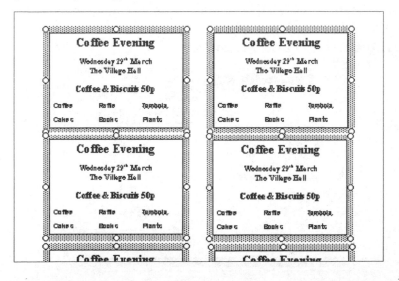

Using Ready-Made Templates

If you want to obtain some quick results, you can use a Word *template*. Whenever you type a Word document it's based on a template, usually the **Normal** or **Blank Document** template provided by default. This sets up the various page details including the margins and font style and size, etc.

However, you can also base a document on a more elaborate template which is really a complete ready-made page including text and graphics. There are libraries of such templates on the Internet covering almost every conceivable occasion or purpose; there are templates for greetings cards, special occasions such as birthdays and all sorts of business and educational stationery.

The basic idea is that you open a new document in Word with a selected template, then modify the text to suit your particular requirements. The advantage of the template is that the art and design features have already been done for you. For example, to make a birthday card, you could open the template shown below and change **Robert** to the name of your friend or relative, etc. (Unless of course their name is Robert). All of the text is in separate text boxes and can easily be edited as shown earlier.

Using an Existing Template to Create a Document

To start a new document based on an existing template already stored on your hard disc, select **File** and **New...** from the Word Menu Bar. The **New Document** Task Pane opens up on the right of the screen and includes the **New from template** extract shown on the right. Clicking on **General Templates....** shown right opens up your **Templates** folder, as shown below.

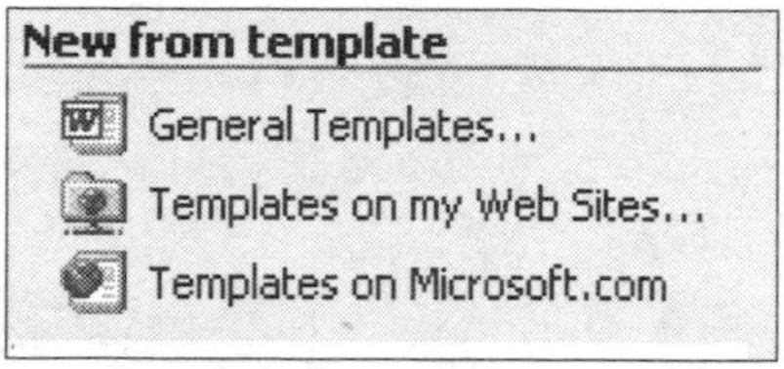

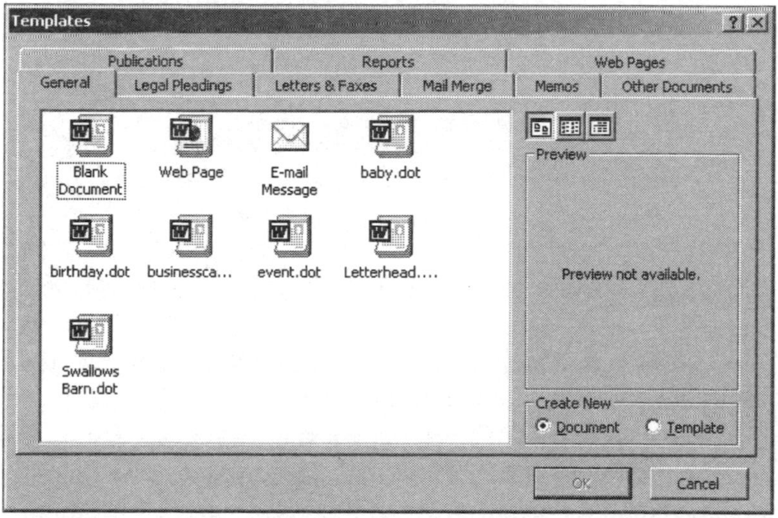

Blank Document, Web Page and **E-mail Message** shown above are all templates provided in Microsoft Word. **Letterhead...** and **Swallows Barn.dot** are templates for headed note paper as discussed on page 103. The templates **birthday.dot**, **baby.dot** and **event.dot** have been downloaded from the **Microsoft Office Template Gallery** on the Internet. Downloading templates is discussed shortly.

Referring to the **Templates** folder shown on page 161, select the template you wish to use, such as **baby.dot**, and click **OK**. Microsoft Word opens up displaying the selected template, as shown below.

The template includes a space and instructions for inserting a photograph. The names and other text are all in separate text boxes which can be selected and edited as discussed previously. Once you have edited the template, the page is then saved as a normal **Word Document** with the file name extension **.doc**. (Unlike a **Document Template** which is saved with the file name extension **.dot**.)

Downloading Templates from the Internet

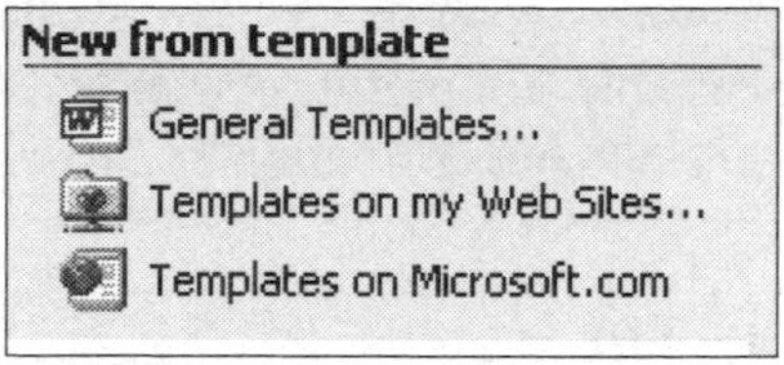

When you select **File** and **New...** from the Word Menu bar, one of the options on the **New Document** Task Pane,

New from template
- General Templates...
- Templates on my Web Sites...
- Templates on Microsoft.com

under **New from template** is **Templates on Microsoft.com**, as shown above. If your computer is connected to the Internet, clicking **Templates on Microsoft.com** opens up the Web site **Microsoft Office Templates Gallery**. This is a library of online templates which can be downloaded and saved on your hard disc, where they can be used to create Word documents.

BROWSE TEMPLATES

Business and Legal

Business Finance | Legal | Meetings and Projects | More...

Calendars, Labels, Planners, and Stationery

Calendars | Stationery | Schedules and Planners | More...

Education

For Teachers | For Parents | For Students | More...

Healthcare and Wellness

Diet and Exercise | For Providers | InfoPath Medical Forms | More...

Microsoft Office Programs

Word | Excel | PowerPoint | More...

Holidays and Occasions

Greeting Cards | Holidays | Occasions and Events

Home and Community

Community and Fundraising | Families | Health, Diet, and Exercise | More...

Your Career

Resumes | Cover Letters | Interview Letters and Tools | More...

Selecting one of the categories shown on the previous page presents a grid of "thumbnails" or miniatures of the available templates. An extract from the **Easter** section of the **Holidays** collection is shown below.

If you now click on one of the thumbnails shown on the previous page, a full-size edition of the chosen template is displayed, together with a **Download Now** button, as shown below.

Depending on the configuration of your computer, you may have to click a second **Download Now** button before the template is downloaded to your computer. Then it can be opened or saved using the dialogue box shown on the next page.

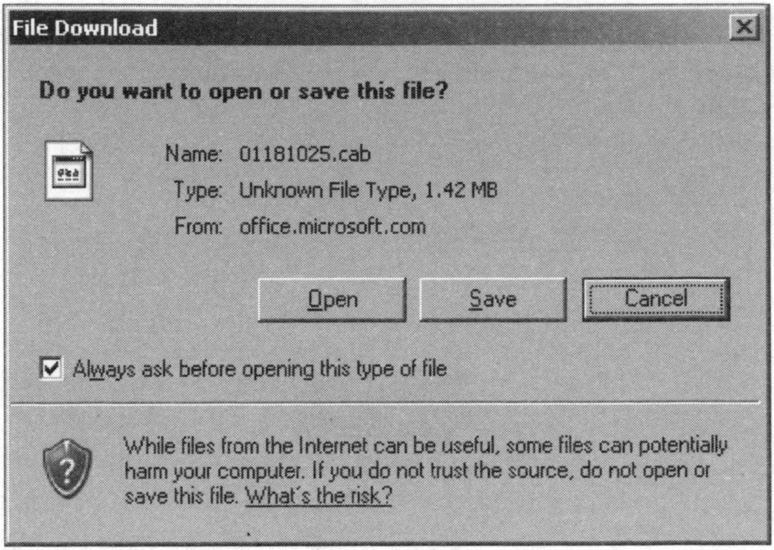

Click the button to **Save** the file; it is initially in a compressed format with the **.cab** (cabinet) file name extension. Select a folder in which to save the compressed file, named **01181025.cab** as shown below. I have created a folder **C:\Office Templates** for this purpose. Creating folders is covered in more detail in Chapter 10.

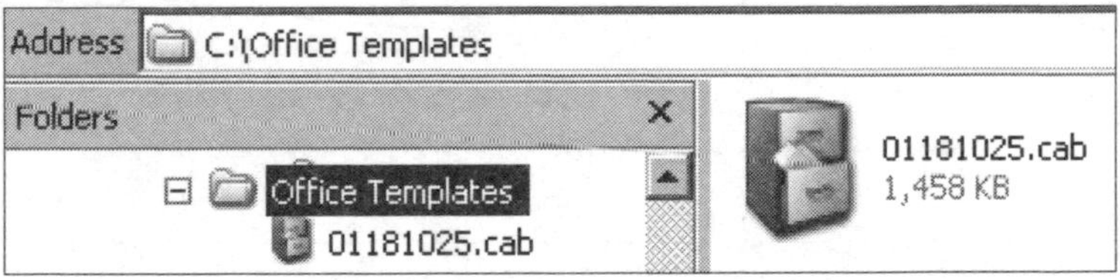

Now open the folder in which this compressed file is saved, **C:\Office Templates** in this example, as shown above and double-click the file.

The file will be expanded into a folder which you must select, as shown on the next page.

I have selected the **Templates** folder in which all of my other templates are saved. In my computer the Word templates are all stored in the folder shown below.

C:\Documents and Settings\Jim\Application Data\Microsoft\Templates

Your templates are probably in the corresponding folder on your computer, except it will be your user name, not **Jim**, after **Documents and Settings** as shown above. Alternatively click **Start** and **Search** and enter **Templates** to search for your templates folder.

Clicking **Extract** shown above expands the compressed file and places a copy of the template into the selected folder. You can see the new template **01181025.dot** alongside the templates discussed earlier, as shown on the next page.

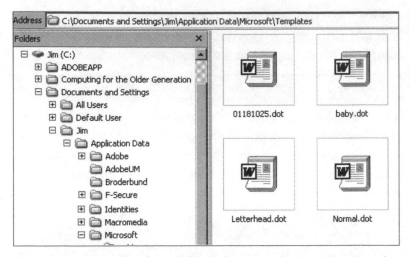

To change to a more meaningful name, such as **Easter**, for example, right-click over the template's icon and select **Rename** fom the resulting menu. Enter the new name **easter.dot** to replace **01181025.dot**.

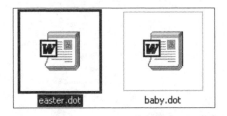

Now to use the new template, open a new blank page in Word using **File** and **New...**. Then from the **New Document** Task Pane on the right of the screen, select **General Templates...** under **New from template**. Your **Templates** folder should open as shown above. Then select the new template and click **OK**. The Word page should open displaying the new template.

Once the Word page has opened with the new template, it becomes an ordinary Word document which can be edited and saved in the normal way.

Please note in this example, the Easter picture appears upside down when the new Word page is opened. This allows any additional messages to be added in text boxes before the card is printed and folded into four to give the finished card shown on the right.

Happy Easter

Templates for Business Cards

The Microsoft Office Template Gallery also includes a set of templates for business cards. These cover various types of business as well as the general card shown below. When you download this template and use it on a new page, as previously described, a table of 10 cards appears, as shown in the extract below. These can be edited on the screen by inserting your own details to replace the text provided. Then print off the business cards in sheets 10 at a time.

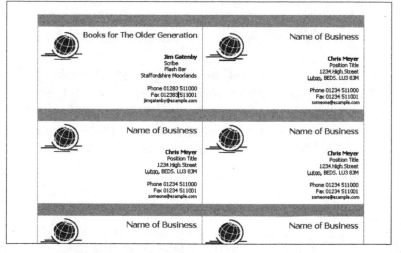

Finding More Templates

If you can't find what you want in the Microsoft Office Template Gallery, try searching the Web by entering **Word templates** using a search program such as Google. You should find lots of templates which you can download, save and customize in the way just described.

That completes our look at the capabilities of Word for manipulating text and graphics to create short single page leaflets, posters, greeting cards, etc. The next chapter looks at the use of Word for the production of longer documents such as booklets, reports, magazines and complete books.

Longer Documents

Introduction

This chapter shows how you can use some of the features in Microsoft Word to help in the production of longer documents such as magazines, newsletters and even complete books like this one. In fact I have used this type of software to produce over 20 books including several of the Older Generation series, of which this book is a part.

Longer documents may use various page layouts and incorporate within the text objects such as pictures, tables, spreadsheets and graphs, etc. Also *headers* and *footers*, which are strips across the top and bottom of the pages in a chapter, into which text such as chapter headings, page numbers, file name and the date can be inserted.

These additional features will enable you to produce longer documents such as, for example:

- A magazine or newsletter about your community
- A booklet describing the history of a village or industry, etc.
- A technical report including tables and graphs
- A business plan for an enterprise you intend to start
- A text book based on the expertise you may have acquired during your working life
- The best-selling novel you always wanted to write.

Page Layouts for Various Documents

This will obviously vary depending on the type of publication, but the starting point is the **Page Setup** dialogue box obtained by clicking **File** and **Page Setup...** on the Word Menu Bar. The **Page Setup** dialogue box below shows the settings used for this particular book. The **Preview** panel at the bottom right below shows the effects of changing any of the **Page Setup** settings.

Using Mirror Margins in a Book Format

The margins of **17 mm**, **18 mm** and **12 mm** shown below and on the previous page were part of the original page design specified by the publishers for this book.

Being a book, larger margins are required at the centre to allow for the binding, so **Mirror margins** has been selected from the drop-down menu shown on the right and on the previous page. The result of this layout is shown below.

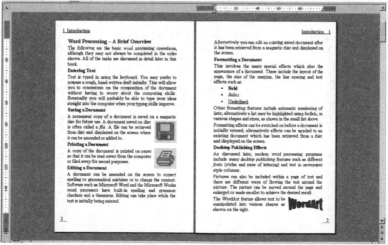

Producing A Folded Booklet

It's often convenient to produce a booklet with two pages of the booklet on one sheet of paper. This is achieved using the **Book fold** option in Word. From the **Page Setup** dialogue box select **Book fold** as shown on the right. After printing, fold

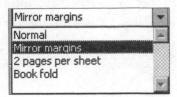

the paper so that it opens like a book. You can print a **Book fold** document on both sides by switching on (with a tick) the **Manual duplex** option in the print dialogue box.

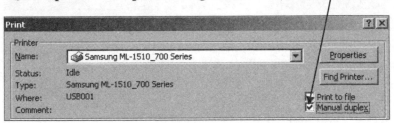

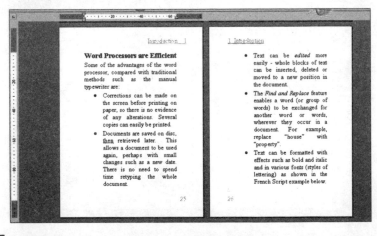

All of the pages on one side of the paper will be printed first then you will be prompted by Word to turn the paper over to print the remaining pages.

Using a Gutter for a Ring Bound Document

If you intend to present a document in a ring or spiral binder, you can use a **Gutter** to add extra space down the left-hand side or along the top side of the paper. This will prevent the binding from overlapping the document.

In this example, a gutter of **25 mm** has been set down the left-hand side of the page, as shown in the **Preview** below, extracted from the **Page Setup** dialogue box shown previously. The gutter is shown chequered down the left-hand side of the preview page.

You can also see from the drop-down menu above, that changes to a document can be applied to the **Whole document** or from **This point forward**.

Setting the Paper Size

For most word processing work you will probably use the **A4** paper size which is standard in the United Kingdom. You may find the paper size specified in your word processor has been set by default at the **Letter** size, which is slightly different from **A4**. To make sure your word processor is set at a particular size, select **File** and **Page Setup...** as before and select the **Paper** tab, as shown below.

When you click the arrow at the right of the **Paper size:** bar, the drop-down menu shown above appears, from which you can select **A4** or whatever size you require. Click **OK** to apply the **Paper size:**.

Setting Your Own Custom Paper Size

If you scroll further down the previous drop-down menu there are many different options for the paper size, including **Custom size**, shown below.

Custom size allows you to specify your own paper size in terms of **Width** and **Height**. The units of measurement, such as **mm** used in this example, are those selected in Word as discussed on page 101 of this book.

For this particular series of books a non-standard paper size of **130.5** mm x **198** mm is used and this is set in the **Paper** tab of the **Page Setup** dialogue box as shown below.

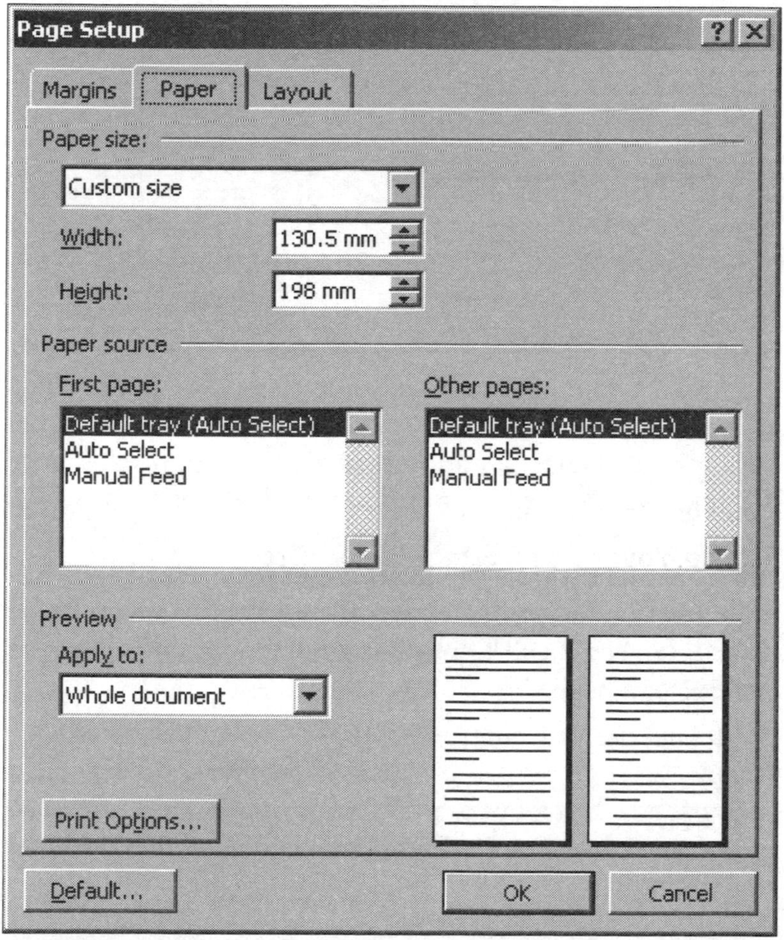

Page Numbers

A substantial booklet, magazine, report or text book, etc., needs numbered pages, enabling you to refer to material on other pages and to create contents and index pages.

To insert page numbers in a document, select **Insert** and **Page Numbers...** from the Word Menu Bar. The **Page Numbers** dialogue box appears as shown below.

You can choose between **Bottom of page (Footer)** and **Top of page (Header)** for the **Position** of the page number. Headers and footers are discussed shortly, but briefly these are lines across the top and bottom of the page in which you can place text such as chapter headings and numbers and page numbers, as shown on the pages of this book. The **Alignment** option shown above allows page numbers to be placed on the **Left, Center, Right**, or on the **Inside** or **Outside** of a page.

By default the page numbering of a document starts at page **1**; however, if you use a separate document to represent each of the chapters of a book, for example, then you need to start the second and subsequent chapters with a different page number.

You can set the starting number for a page in the **Page Numbers** dialogue box, after clicking the **Format...** button, shown on the previous page. In the example below, a chapter has been set to **Start at** page **137**.

There are further options for the page numbers, such as to include the chapter number with the page number as in **1-1**, **1-2**, etc., and also different page number formats, such as Roman numerals and letters instead of numbers.

Headers and Footers

These are used in longer documents and allow a title or chapter heading and information such as the page number, document name or date to be added along the top or bottom of the pages in a document.

For example, on the pages of this book, the chapter title, e.g. 9 Longer Documents, has been set up as a header. The page number has been set up as a footer.

From the word processor Menu Bar, select **View** and **Header and Footer**. Empty boxes for the header and footer appear on the page.

```
,_Header_____
¦3   Walking in the Lake District
¦
L_____
```

You can type your own text freely into the header and footer boxes, as shown above. Or you can use the header and footer toolbar, shown below, to insert current information onto the page. The toolbar appears automatically on the screen, after you click **View** and **Header and Footer**. This allows you to insert information in the header and footer on the pages throughout a document.

```
Header and Footer
    Insert AutoText ▾    # ⅙ ⅚   ⊡ ⊘   ⬚ ⬚   ⬚   ⬚ ⬚ ⬚   Close
```

The above toolbar allows you to insert information in both the header and the footer. An icon towards the right of the toolbar allows you to switch between the header and the footer.

A drop-down menu obtained by clicking the arrow to the right of **Insert AutoText** on the **Header and Footer** toolbar displays a wealth of information which can be inserted automatically in the headers or footers throughout the document.

Header and Footer

Insert AutoText ▾

- PAGE -
Author, Page #, Date
Confidential, Page #, Date
Created by
Created on
Filename
Filename and path
Last printed
Last saved by
Page X of Y

Moving along the toolbar shown above, the next three icons allow you to **Insert Page Number**, **Insert Number of Pages** and **Format Page Number** as discussed earlier in this chapter.

The next two icons on the toolbar allow you to enter the **Date** and **Time** in the header or footer.

The next icon on the toolbar opens the **Page Setup** dialogue box discussed earlier, which appears open at the **Layout** tab as shown on the next page.

The **Page Setup** dialogue box open at the **Layout** tab below shows the settings for the headers and footers used in this particular book.

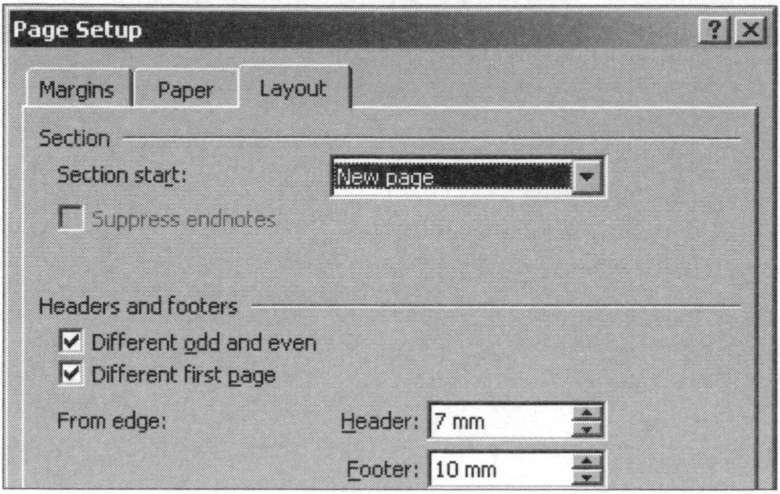

Page Setup	? X

Margins   **Paper**   **Layout**

Section
   Section sta<u>r</u>t: New page   ▼
    ☐ Suppress endnotes

Headers and footers
    ☑ Different <u>o</u>dd and even
    ☑ Different first <u>p</u>age

From edge: <u>H</u>eader: 7 mm   ▲▼
                               <u>F</u>ooter: 10 mm   ▲▼

As shown above the **Page Setup** dialogue box allows you to set the distances of the headers and footers from the edge of the paper. Under **Headers and footers** shown above **Different odd and even** has been switched on with a tick. As you can see at the top of the pages of this book, the header is on the left on the even pages and on the right on the odd pages.

Different first page has also been switched on in the above **Page Setup** dialogue box. This is because the header is not required on the first, i.e. title page, of each chapter in this book.

After you have inserted the required information using the icons on the **Headers and footers** toolbar shown previously, click **Close**. The selected information will now appear in the headers and footers throughout the document.

Inserting a Table

From the **Table** menu on the word processor menu bar, select **Insert** and **Table**.... The following dialogue box appears:

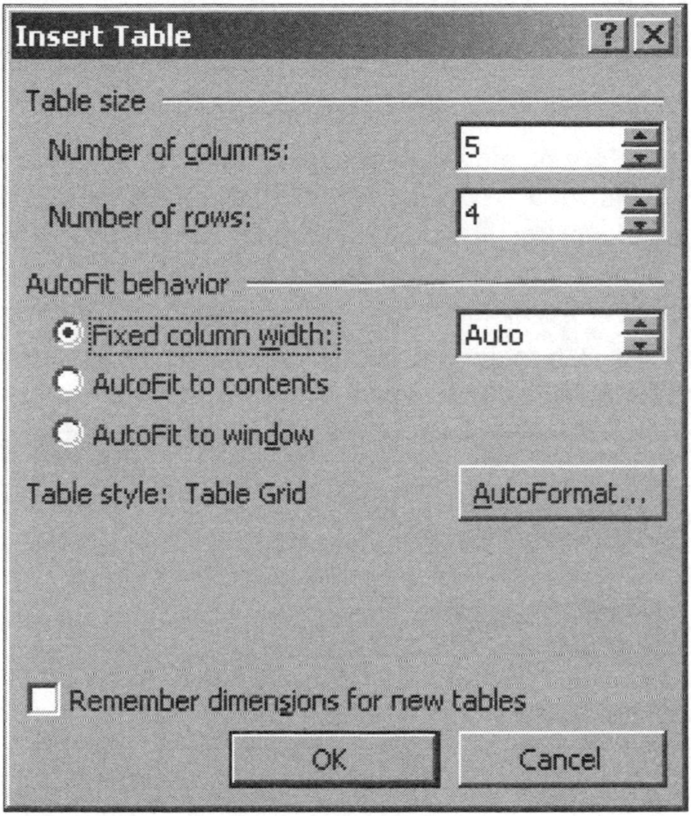

Insert Table   ? X

Table size

Number of columns: 5

Number of rows: 4

AutoFit behavior

◉ Fixed column width: Auto

○ AutoFit to contents

○ AutoFit to window

Table style: Table Grid   AutoFormat...

☐ Remember dimensions for new tables

OK   Cancel

You specify the number of vertical columns and horizontal rows, as shown above and click **OK** to insert the table in your document, as shown on the next page. The top left-hand corner of the table is placed at the current cursor position.

The cursor appears in the top left-hand box or *cell*, ready for you to start entering the headings and data.

The table can be moved by dragging the small square at the top left shown above. The table can be resized by dragging the small square shown at the bottom right above. Words and numbers are typed straight into the cells in the table. To move to a cell, click in the cell or use the cursor keys.

The cells in a table can be selected and edited using the drop-down **Table** menu shown below.

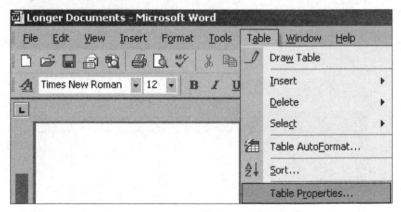

In the **Table** menu shown above, **Table Properties...** allows you to set the alignment of the table **Left**, **Right** and **Center**. You can also set the way the text in the main document wraps around the table. The row height and column width of an existing table can be altered and rows and columns can added and deleted.

In the **Table** menu shown on the previous page, the **Table AutoFormat...** option presents a choice of ready-made styles of table, incorporating different fonts and background shading. The **Table AutoFormat** can be applied before a new table is inserted or an existing table can be selected and a new **AutoFormat** applied, as shown below.

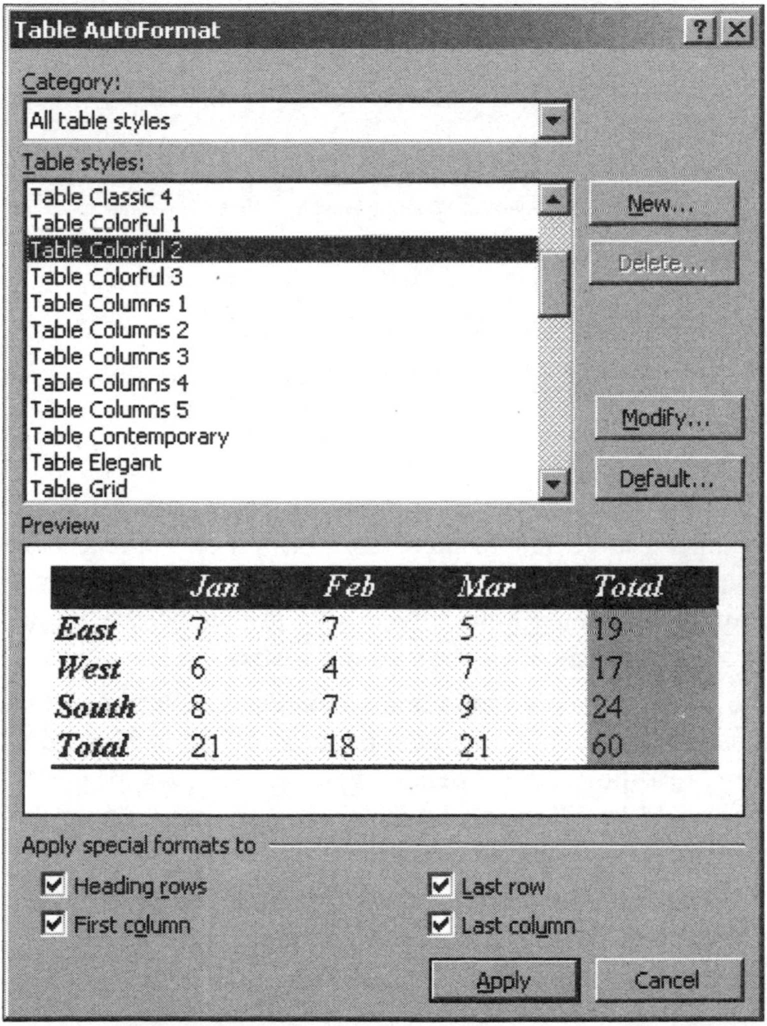

Table AutoFormat	? X

Category:

All table styles ▼

Table styles:

Table Classic 4	New...
Table Colorful 1	
Table Colorful 2	Delete...
Table Colorful 3	
Table Columns 1	
Table Columns 2	
Table Columns 3	
Table Columns 4	
Table Columns 5	Modify...
Table Contemporary	
Table Elegant	Default...
Table Grid	

Preview

	Jan	Feb	Mar	Total
East	7	7	5	19
West	6	4	7	17
South	8	7	9	24
Total	21	18	21	60

Apply special formats to

☑ Heading rows ☑ Last row
☑ First column ☑ Last column

Apply   Cancel

Copying a Spreadsheet into a Word Document

A spreadsheet program like Microsoft Excel is used to do calculations on tables of figures. A simple spreadsheet for calculating household spending in a fictitious household is shown below.

	A	B	C	D	E	F	G	H
1								
2			Weekly Spending					
3								
4		Week 1	Week 2	Week 3	Week 4	Total	Average	
5								
6	Food	42.65	37.97	46.41	48.57	175.60	43.90	
7	Heating	19.28	21.42	23.42	21.48	85.60	21.40	
8	Electricity	9.47	11.97	10.97	12.01	44.42	11.11	
9	Rent	85.00	85.00	85.00	85.00	340.00	85.00	
10	Petrol	17.27	18.43	21.57	20.87	78.14	19.54	
11	Car	19.00	17.00	21.49	26.93	84.42	21.11	
12	Total	192.67	191.79	208.86	214.86	808.18	202.05	
13								

It's often useful, when writing a report as a Word document, to be able to include all or part of a spreadsheet within the text of the report. For example, if you were campaigning for a new bypass you might include in the report a spreadsheet giving traffic statistics.

The method for incorporating a spreadsheet into a Word document is given on the next page. You will need to have the spreadsheet table open in your spreadsheet program. This could be Microsoft Excel or the spreadsheet program in Microsoft Works, for example.

More details of creating spreadsheets is given in our book "Computing for the Older Generation" from Bernard Babani (publishing) Ltd.

First select the area of the spreadsheet you wish to copy into Word. This is done by dragging the mouse (keeping the left-hand button held down) over the required cells. This highlights the required area with a coloured background as shown shaded below.

Microsoft Excel - Household spending						
File Edit View Insert Format Tools Data Window Help						
A2		fx				
A	B	C	D	E	F	G
1						
2		Weekly Spending				
3						
4	Week 1	Week 2	Week 3	Week 4	Total	Average
5						
6 Food	42.65	37.97	46.41	48.57	175.60	43.90
7 Heating	19.28	21.42	23.42	21.48	85.60	21.40
8 Electricity	9.47	11.97	10.97	12.01	44.42	11.11
9 Rent	85.00	85.00	85.00	85.00	340.00	85.00
10 Petrol	17.27	18.43	21.57	20.87	78.14	19.54
11 Car	19.00	17.00	21.49	26.93	84.42	21.11
12 Total	192.67	191.79	208.86	214.86	808.18	202.05
13						

Now select **Edit** and **Copy** from the spreadsheet Menu Bar. The copy command places a copy of the selected spreadsheet cells onto the Windows *clipboard*. The clipboard is a temporary store in the computer's memory.

Next, switch to Word and place the cursor at the position in the document or report where you want the top left-hand corner of the spreadsheet extract to appear. Now select **Edit** and **Paste** to place a copy of the spreadsheet extract in the Word document, as shown on the next page.

Cutting, copying and pasting using the clipboard are discussed in more detail in Appendix 1.

	Weekly Spending					
	Week 1	Week 2	Week 3	Week 4	Total	Average
Food	42.65	37.97	46.41	48.57	175.60	43.90
Heating	19.28	21.42	23.42	21.48	85.60	21.40
Electricity	9.47	11.97	10.97	12.01	44.42	11.11
Rent	85.00	85.00	85.00	85.00	340.00	85.00
Petrol	17.27	18.43	21.57	20.87	78.14	19.54
Car	19.00	17.00	21.49	26.93	84.42	21.11
Total	192.67	191.79	208.86	214.86	808.18	202.05

The spreadsheet extract can be moved around the Word page by dragging the small square containing four arrows at the top left-hand corner. Use this to place the spreadsheet extract in its final position.

The spreadsheet extract can be resized by dragging the small square at the bottom right-hand corner.

.14	19.54
.42	21.11
18	202.05

A graph or chart produced in a spreadsheet program or an extract from a database can be copied into a Word document using **Edit**, **Copy** and **Paste** in a similar way to that just described for a spreadsheet extract.

Word Count

If your document is restricted to a certain number of words, as in the case of an article for publication, for example, there is an automatic word count facility in Word, accessed off **Tools** and **Word Count**....

Word Count

Statistics:

Pages	17
Words	2,084
Characters (no spaces)	9,536
Characters (with spaces)	11,564
Paragraphs	76
Lines	284

☐ Include footnotes and endnotes

Show Toolbar   Close

Getting Printed and Published

Whether you intend to produce a few hundred copies of a magazine aimed at your local community or a book selling thousands of copies for world-wide publication, you are unlikely to be able to print and bind the copies yourself. At the very least you will need to use a local printing firm. The next two pages outline some of my experience of producing text ready to send to a printing company.

While the world in general has adopted the PC standard using Microsoft Windows (and predominantly Microsoft Word), many printers and publishers have favoured the Apple Macintosh computer. This was because for many years the Mac was well ahead of the PC with an easy-to-use windows "user interface" and powerful desktop publishing software such as Aldus Pagemaker. While Microsoft Windows and programs like Microsoft Word have done much to redress the balance for the PC, many printing and publishing firms continue to use the Mac.

Although you can find printing firms who will accept files straight from your PC, this will inevitably limit your choice of company. The solution is to convert your Word files to a standard format which can be handled by any printing company no matter what equipment they use. Such a standard is the Adobe Acrobat PDF or Portable Document Format. This format is also widely used for documents to be downloaded from the Internet. (For downloading and viewing Internet PDF files you need the freely available Adobe Reader software.)

However, to create your own PDF documents to be sent to a printing company, you need to purchase a full copy of the Adobe Acrobat software, which includes a component called Acrobat Distiller.

Adobe Acrobat 4.0	▶	Acrobat Catalog 4.0
Microsoft Works	▶	Acrobat Distiller 4.0
Microsoft Office PowerPoint Viewer 2003		Adobe Acrobat 4.0
Microsoft Word		Register Acrobat 4.0
Microsoft Works Task Launcher		Uninstall Adobe Acrobat 4.0

Once your documents have been edited and proof read in Word, they can be converted to PDF format using Distiller and saved as separate PDF files. Then you can be confident that any printing company should be able to handle your text. Although small alterations are possible using Adobe Acrobat, major editing needs to be done in Word, before you create the final PDF file.

Finding a Publisher for a Book

If you're submitting a speculative book proposal to a publisher, it's normal to send a few sample chapters rather than the complete book. Remember that publishers are inundated with proposals from hopeful authors; if it is to succeed, your magnum opus must stand out from the pile. Make sure you are meticulous in the material you send; sloppy spelling and punctuation will imply a similar cavalier approach to factual accuracy within the text.

If your book is to be commercially printed, the ability to send the finished "manuscript" in PDF format on a CD will enable the printers to *typeset from disc*. This is obviously much more attractive to a publisher than a book sent as a printout on paper which still has to be expensively typeset. A substantial book in PDF format can easily be accommodated on a CD costing a few pence.

For more details of Adobe Acrobat and Distiller please have a look at:

www.adobe.co.uk

Managing Your Word Files

Introduction

It's all very well being able to produce impressive documents embracing all of the stylish effects which Word has to offer. However, unless you can organize and manage your work efficiently and safely, disaster could easily strike. For example, if you accidentally make a mistake while naming and saving a file, an entire document could be lost – not at all funny if the file represents a major effort such as a newsletter, magazine or your autobiography. Fortunately, as discussed in this chapter, there are simple and inexpensive methods of protecting your work.

This chapter looks at methods of saving, managing and protecting your work as follows:

- Naming and saving your work as a file

- Creating a hierarchical system of folders in which to save your work

- Moving, copying, deleting files and folders within the system of folders in the Windows Explorer

- Making backup copies of important work on a CD

- Protecting your computer against viruses or illegal access from the Internet

- Sending a Word document as an e-mail attachment.

Files and Folders

A common cause of frustration is not being able to find a piece of work which you know you saved somewhere on your hard disc. This can be avoided by saving your work in an organized system of folders with meaningful names – just like a traditional filing cabinet. In the following example a folder called **Holidays** has been created on the **C:** drive (the hard disc) and is shown open in the Windows Explorer.

Within the **Holidays** folder shown below is a sub-folder called **Tuscany** and also a file called **Enquiry about Rome**. The file is a letter created and saved in Microsoft Word.

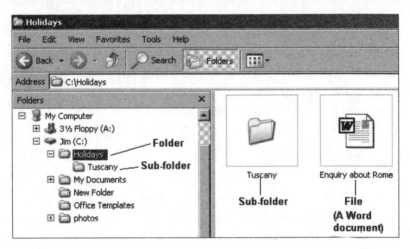

The path name for the letter shown above is:

C:\Holidays\Enquiry about Rome

Creating a New File Using Save As...

Before you start entering the actual text of a document it's a good idea to create a new file with a suitable name on the hard disc. Then it's a simple matter to quickly save the document at intervals while you are entering the text. When you select **File** and **Save As...** from the Word Menu Bar, the following dialogue box appears.

In the **Save As** dialogue box shown above, the **Save in** bar at the top is already displaying a folder, **My Documents**. This is the default folder provided by Windows. You can either leave the folder **My Documents** selected or use the drop-down menu to choose another folder in which to save your work. The drop-down menu also includes any folders which you may have created, as discussed shortly.

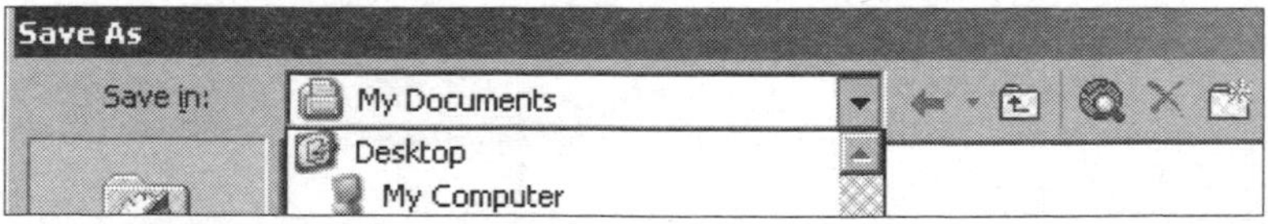

Naming a File

When you open the **Save As:** dialogue box shown on the previous page, the **File name:** bar displays the default name, **Doc3**, in this example, provided by Word.

File name:	Doc3	▼
Save as type:	Word Document	▼

You could continue to use the default file name but it's preferable to use a more meaningful file name of your own. Delete the default name, **Doc3**, and enter your own name (up to 255 characters long) such as **Enquiry about Rome**, for example.

File name:	Enquiry about Rome	▼
Save as type:	Word Document	▼

Now click the **Save** button on the bottom of the **Save As** dialogue box shown on the previous page.

Quick Saves

Once you have saved the document using **Save As**, it now exists as a file on your hard disc, with its own file name. In

the future, whenever you want to save the file with the same name, simply click on the **Save** icon shown left and on the Word toolbar shown below.

File	Edit	View	Insert	Format	Tools	Table	Window

🗋 🗁 🖫 🖨 🔃 | 🖨 🗋 ✓ | ✂ 🖹 🖺 ✐ | ↻ ▾ ↺

🔠 Times New Roman ▾ 12 ▾ **B** *I* U | ≣ ≣ ≣ ≣

Saving Only the Latest Version of a Document

If you keep saving a document with the same name, by clicking the **Save** icon as just described, then as the document develops over a period of time, new versions overwrite, i.e. wipe out, the earlier versions on the hard disc.

Saving Different Versions of a Document

If you want to keep several versions of the same document, save the document with a different name each time using the **Save As...** option off the **File** menu on the Word Toolbar. Enter the new file name as described on the previous page. You might use **Doc1, Doc2, Doc3**, etc., but more meaningful names for each version are preferable.

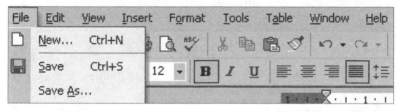

Please note: The **Save** option on the above **File** menu has the same effect as clicking the **Save** icon on the Toolbar.

Saving Long Documents

When working on a long document it makes sense to save the document regularly – you wouldn't want to lose several hours' work if there's a power cut, for example. I avoid this problem by clicking the **Save** icon on the Toolbar every 10 minutes or so. You can also set Word to **Save AutoRecover info : 10 minutes**, say, after selecting **Tools, Options...** and the **Save** tab from the Word Menu bar.

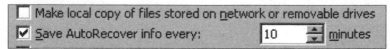

Creating a New Folder

Using the Save As Dialogue Box

Note that by default a document is saved as a file in the Windows folder **My Documents**, unless you've selected another folder. You can create a new folder within the folder **My Documents** after clicking the icon shown right and also shown below in the extract from the **Save As** dialogue box.

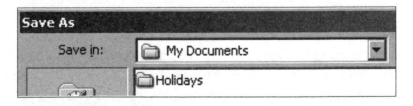

The **New Folder** dialogue box appears, as shown below, in which you enter the name of your new folder.

Please note that the new folder, **Holidays** in this example, has been created in the folder **My Documents**, as this was the folder currently selected in the **Save As** dialogue box shown below.

Creating a New Folder Using the Windows Explorer

Instead of using the **Save As** dialogue box, you can create new folders in the Windows Explorer. This will help you to see how the new folders fit into the overall hierarchy or structure of folders on your hard disc.

First we might create a folder for word processing documents on the **C:** drive. In this folder, called **word processing,** we will create a sub-folder called **letters**.

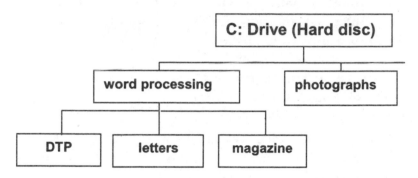

Open up the Windows Explorer by right-clicking over the **Start** button at the bottom left of the screen. Select **Explore** from the menu which pops up. Highlight the **C:** drive and select **File, New** and **Folder** from the Explorer Menu Bar as shown below.

A box containing the words **New Folder** appears in the right-hand panel of Explorer, as shown below.

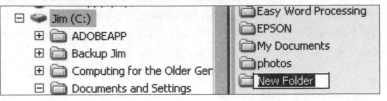

Delete the words **New Folder** and enter the name of your new folder, in this case **word processing**. When you press

the **Enter** key the new folder **word processing** will be added to the list of folders on the **C:** drive, as shown on the right. (The plus signs indicate folders which contain sub-folders.)

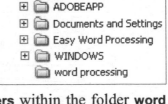

To create a sub-folder called **letters** within the folder **word processing**, highlight the folder **word processing** in the

Windows Explorer. Now select **File**, **New** and **Folder** from the Menu Bar as before. The **New Folder** icon appears in the right-hand panel as before.

Enter the name **letters** and press **Enter** to create the new folder. The new folder **letters** is a sub-folder within the folder **word processing** on the **C:** drive. A minus sign indicates a folder open to show its files and sub-folders.

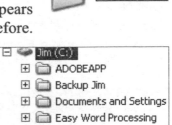

The path name to this folder is:

C:\word processing\letters

Saving a Word File in a New Folder

Whenever you want to save a Word document in a folder that you have created, simply click **File** and **Save As:** from the Word Menu Bar as shown below.

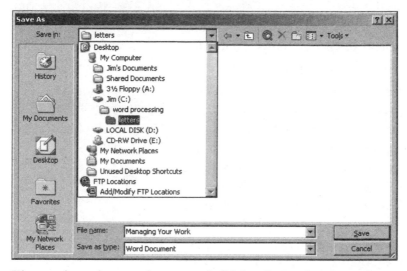

Then select the newly-created folder from the drop-down menu next to **Save in:** as shown below. Finally click the **Save** button as shown at the bottom right above.

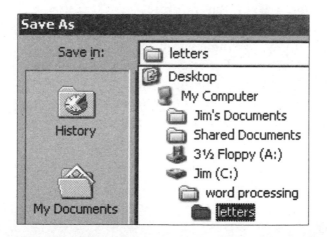

Common File and Folder Tasks

The Windows Explorer enables you to manage your files and folders. This includes moving files and folders to other folders within the hierarchy and renaming and deleting files and folders. Many of these tasks can also be carried out using the **File and Folder Tasks** pane in Windows XP and this is discussed in detail later in this chapter.

Renaming Files and Folders

Start Explorer by right-clicking over the **Start** button and selecting **Explore** from the pop-up menu. A folder or file can be renamed by right-clicking over its name or icon in the Windows Explorer, then selecting **Rename** from the menu which appears (shown on the right). Alternatively the folder or file name can be highlighted, followed by selection of **File** and **Rename** from the Menu Bar across the top of the Explorer window. The folder or file name appears in a rectangle with a flashing cursor. Rename the folder or file by deleting the existing name and typing in the new one, then press the **Enter** or **Return** key.

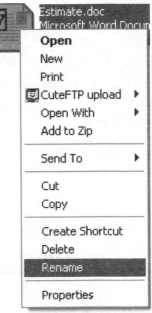

Deleting Files and Folders

Highlight the file or folder in the Windows Explorer then press the **Delete** key. Or you can select **Delete** from the **File** menu. (The **File** menu can be selected from the Menu Bar or by right-clicking over the file or folder). When you delete a folder in Windows XP then all of the subfolders and files contained within are also deleted, i.e. moved to the **Recycle Bin**. Some earlier versions of Windows require a folder to be empty before it can be deleted.

Using the File and Folder Tasks Menu to Delete Files and Folders

If the **File and Folder Tasks** menu is not displayed, select **View, Explorer Bar** and click the word **Folders** in the drop-down menu to remove the tick. Highlight the file or folder and select **Delete this file** from the **File and Folder Tasks** menu on the left of the screen, as shown below.

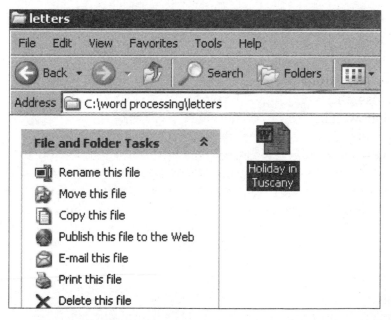

Undoing a Delete Operation

If you make a mistake and delete the wrong folders or files, you can use the **Undo Delete** option in the **Edit** menu (provided you spot the mistake straightaway.) Fortunately files and folders are not lost forever when they are deleted. Windows XP merely transfers them to its **Recycle Bin**.

The Recycle Bin

The **Recycle Bin** is invoked by clicking its icon on the Windows Desktop. It is effectively a folder into which all deleted files are initially sent. As shown below, you can view the contents of the Recycle Bin at any time by clicking its icon on the Windows Desktop.

Once in the Recycle Bin files and folders can be left for a time, but as they are still taking up hard disc space they should eventually be permanently deleted using **Empty the Recycle Bin** shown above. **Restore all items** shown above returns all files and folders from the Recycle Bin to their original location on the hard disc.

Moving and Copying Files and Folders

The following tasks are described in the context of files, but the methods apply equally to folders.

Moving a file deletes the file from its original location and places it in a new location.

Copying a file places a replica of the file in a new location and leaves the original edition of the file in the original location.

Files can be copied or moved between different locations on the same hard disc, between two hard discs in the same computer or between different media such as a hard disc and a CD.

Dragging and Dropping

With the required files and folders displayed in the Windows Explorer, a common copying method is to drag the file or folder with the mouse and drop it over the new location. Different results are obtained depending on whether you are dragging and dropping to the same or a different medium:

- The file is *moved* if it is dragged and dropped into a different location on the same hard disc.

- The file is *copied* if it is dragged and dropped onto a different disc such as a CD or floppy disc, etc.

To *copy* files within the same hard disc the **Control** key (marked **Ctrl**) must be held down while dragging with the left-hand mouse button continuously held down.

You can copy between different locations on the main hard disc drive **C:** or to and from any other drives such as the floppy disc or CD.

Open the Windows Explorer and make sure the folders or files you wish to copy or move are visible in the right-hand panel. If you can't see the resources such as the hard disc (**C:**), CD drive (usually **D**: or **E**;), etc., in the left-hand panel as shown below, select **View**, **Explorer Bar** and make sure **Folders** is ticked.

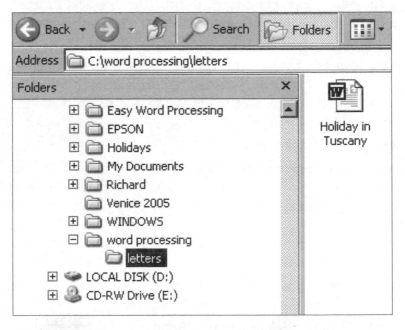

Now highlight the file(s) or folder(s) to be copied or moved. (To highlight multiple files and folders, hold down the **Ctrl** key continuously while clicking with the mouse.) Next hold down the left-hand button and drag the highlighted files and/or folders to their destination in the left-hand panel. Release the mouse button to drop the files into the new location. This method would typically be used to copy some files onto a floppy disc or CD in order to transfer the files to another computer.

Using the Right-hand Mouse Button to Copy or Move Files and Folders

Drag the icon for a file or folder using the right-hand button on the mouse, then release the button to drop the file or folder over its new location. The menu on the right appears, allowing you to copy or move the file or folder.

Copy Here
Move Here
Create Shortcuts Here

Cancel

Copying, Cutting and Pasting Using the Edit Menu

You can also copy and move files in the Windows Explorer by using the **Edit** menu. Select the file or folder then use **Edit** and either **Copy** or **Cut** to place the file or folder on the Windows clipboard. Now select the destination folder and use **Edit** and **Paste** to place the file or folder in the destination folder.

Using the File and Folder Tasks Menu to Copy or Move Files and Folders

The **File and Folder Tasks** pane, shown below, can be switched on and off in Explorer by clicking **View, Explorer Bar** and **Folders**.

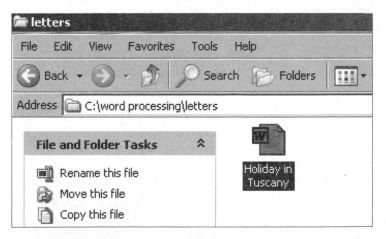

Please note that the Windows Explorer displays the appropriate menu in the **File and Folder Tasks** pane according to whether a file or a folder has been selected in the right-hand pane of Explorer. This is shown in the two panes below.

Moving or copying is made easy with special **Copy Items** and **Move Items** windows appearing when either **Move this file** (or **folder**) or **Copy this file** (or **folder**) are selected. As shown above the same method is used for both *files* and *folders*, depending which has been highlighted in Explorer. The **Move Items** window (shown below) and the **Copy Items** window allow the destination to be selected.

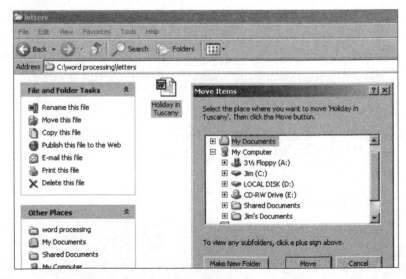

For example, the file called **Holiday in Tuscany**, shown highlighted on the previous page, is to be moved. **Move this file** is selected from the **File and Folder Tasks** pane on the left. Then the **Move Items** dialogue box appears enabling you to select the destination for the file or folder being moved. This could be another folder on the **C:** drive, a floppy disc or writeable CD in drive **D:** or **E:**. Click the **Move** button shown below to complete the operation. The **Copy** process is carried out in a similar way.

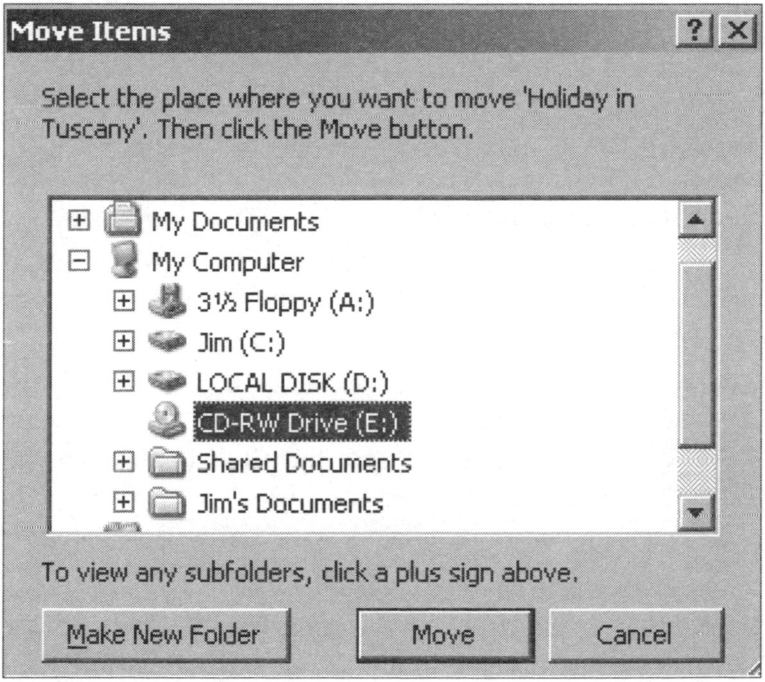

Warning!! Moving, copying, deleting and renaming of files and folders should only be applied to the files and folders you have created – never to the Windows and other program files essential to the functioning of your computer.

Backing Up Your Work to a CD

The Need for Backups

It often seems a nuisance to have to stop work to make a duplicate copy of important files. However, I have heard of two people who each lost the best part of a year's work through not making backup copies. Using the simple methods described in this chapter I have been able to produce over 20 books without ever losing any work at all.

New computers are generally equipped with CD drives capable of writing files to a blank CD. The CD is an excellent and cost-effective backup medium. There are two main types of writeable CD, the CD-R and the CD-RW. The CD-R can be written to only once. The CD-RW can be written to many times. I use the CD-R for backup work, for the following reasons:

- The CD-R can cost as little as 10p at the time of writing, especially if you buy a pack of 100 or more.

- The CD has a storage capacity of nearly 700MB, compared with the meager 1.44MB of the floppy disc. You can easily store the equivalent of several books, like this one, on one CD.

- CDs in my experience are extremely reliable, accurate and virtually indestructible.

Although my main backup medium is the CD, I also make interim backups several times a day onto a second hard drive fitted inside of the computer, to save accumulating too many CDs. This is a fast and reliable method and means that at most I can only lose a few minutes work. One disadvantage of relying solely on a second hard disc would be that the work would be lost if the computer was stolen.

Each week I copy all of my work (i.e. the current book project) from my hard disc onto a CD-R. You could do a backup every day but this creates a lot of CDs to handle.

Obviously it's important to have an efficient system of labelling and storing your backup media in a secure place. Backup copies of important work should be kept in a separate location away from any risk of fire, theft, or flooding, etc.

For peace of mind, after backing up important files, it's always a good idea to check that the backup was successful. Try opening the backed up files from the backup media. This can be done using **File** and **Open...** or by double-clicking the file names or icons in the **Windows Explorer** as discussed shortly.

The Storage Capacity of a CD

As an indication of the storage capacity of a CD, I have put several of my Older Generation books onto one CD. Each of the six books is in the form of Word files representing nearly 1400 pages of text and graphics.

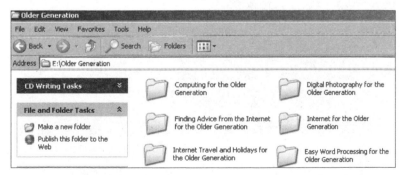

These 6 books in total only take up a fraction of the CD's storage space – 226MB out of a total capacity of 680MB – not bad for a CD costing less than 20 pence.

Making a CD Backup

There are several programs for copying files and folders to a CD. For a long time I have used the CD "burning" facility built into Windows XP; it is easy to use and has always been reliable.

To make a CD backup, first place a blank CD in the drive. A small dialogue box appears, from which you select **Take no action** and click **OK**.

There are several ways to proceed from now but I find the **Send To** option quick and easy to use. Open the Windows Explorer by right-clicking over the **Start** menu and selecting **Explore** from the menu which pops up. Now select the file and/or folders to copy to the CD by left-clicking. To select more than one file or folder hold down the **Ctrl** key while clicking with the mouse. When the required files and/or folders are highlighted, right-click one of them. This causes a menu to appear which includes the **Send To** option. From the menu shown below, select **CD Drive (E:)** or possibly **CD Drive (D:)**, depending on your computer's configuration.

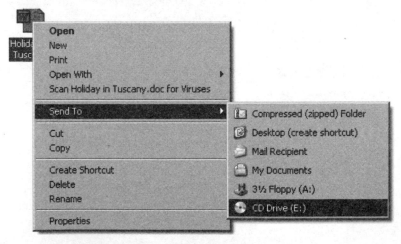

A balloon appears at the bottom of the screen informing you that **You have files to be written to the CD**.

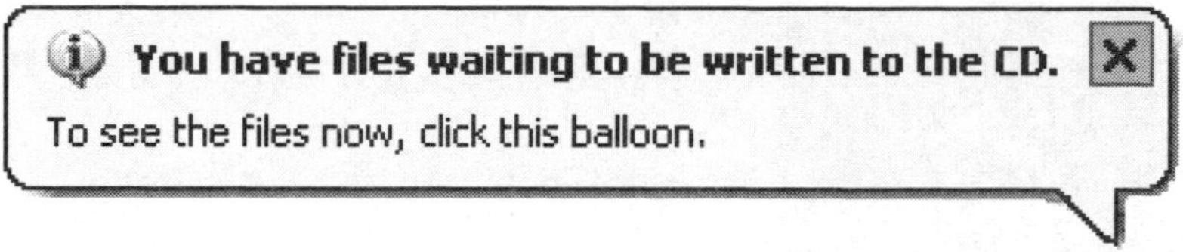

Click anywhere inside of the balloon and a window appears displaying **Files Ready to Be Written to the CD** as shown below.

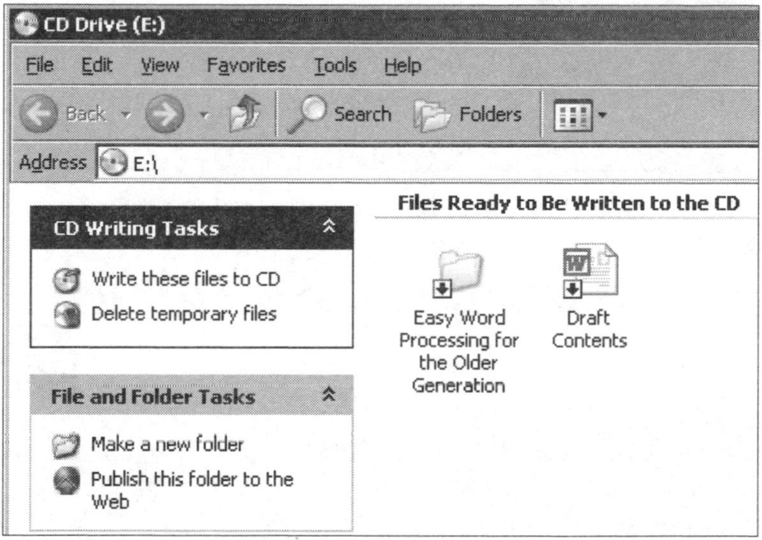

Now click **Write these files to CD** from the **CD Writing Tasks** menu shown on the left-hand side above. This starts the **CD Writing Wizard** shown on the next page, where you are able to give a name to the CD (if you don't want to use the current date supplied by default as the CD name).

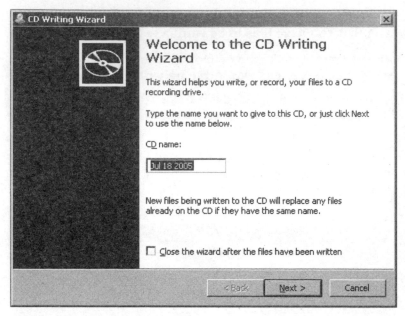

After clicking **Next** a window appears showing the progress being made in the copying process.

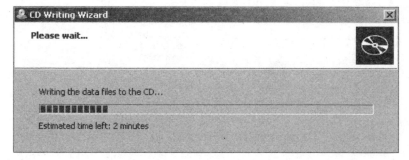

When the files have been copied, another window appears telling you that the copying process has been successful. Click **Finish** to complete the backup process. The CD should now be labelled and stored in a safe place.

Recovering Files from a Backup CD or Disc

If you ever need to restore the files you've backed up onto CD (or floppy disc), place the CD in the drive and use the standard **File** and **Open...** commands which appear on the Word Menu Bar. Select the CD drive (usually **(D:)** or **(E:)**)from the drop-down menu in the **Look in:** bar shown below. Then browse to find and select the file you want and click the **Open** button.

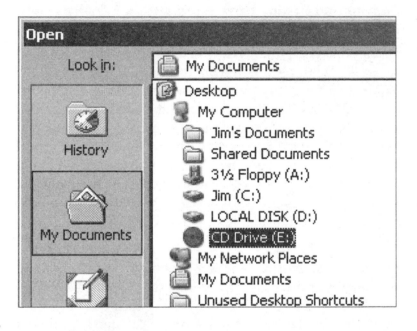

Another way to open a file from a CD (or any other disc) is to display the file name in the Windows Explorer. Now double-click the name of the file or its icon. In the case of a Word file, the Word program will be launched with the chosen document open and ready for reading or editing.

Sending a Word Document with an E-mail

The e-mail is a very fast and convenient way of communicating with friends and relatives or business colleagues. A brief message can be typed straight into an e-mail program such as Microsoft Outlook Express or MSN Hotmail. However, you may want to send a longer document to a friend or colleague – perhaps to obtain their opinion on something you have written, for example.

Copying and Pasting from Word into an E-mail

For a small amount of text and pictures it may be possible to copy material from Word and paste it into the e-mail message. With the document open in Word, select the required text and any graphics then use **Edit** and **Copy** off the Word Menu Bar. Next switch to the e-mail program and display the page for creating a message. Now use **Edit** and **Paste** in the e-mail program to embed the copied text and any graphics into the e-mail message. (Cutting, copying and pasting are discussed in detail earlier in Appendix 1). You should be able to edit the text pasted into the e-mail program and type further text, if necessary.

E-mail Attachments

For longer documents it is not feasible to copy and paste text and graphics into the e-mail message. The e-mail *attachment* enables complete files such as a Word document, to be sent by e-mail. The attached file is "clipped" onto an outgoing e-mail message and sent along with the e-mail to the required destination e-mail address. When someone receives an e-mail with an attached file, the message and the attachment can be downloaded to their computer. The recipient can then view the attachment in the appropriate program such as Microsoft Word.

Creating an E-mail Attachment

For this exercise a copy of the Venice leaflet discussed earlier will be prepared as an e-mail attachment. First the e-mail program is opened up and the recipient's e-mail address and a **Subject:** are entered. Then the accompanying text of the message is entered. The example below uses the Outlook Express program.

```
Leaflet on Venice

File  Edit  View  Insert  Format  Tools  Message  Help

  Send    Cut   Copy  Paste  Undo   Check Spelling  Attach Priority   Sig

  To:    andrewgatenby@egtonbridge.com
  Cc:
  Subject:  Leaflet on Venice

  Arial          14    B  I  U  A

  Andrew

  I thought you might be interested in the attached leaflet.

  Your comments would be appreciated.
```

Next click the **Attach** (paper-clip) icon off the Outlook Express Menu Bar. This opens up the **Insert Attachment** dialogue box shown on the next page.

Attach

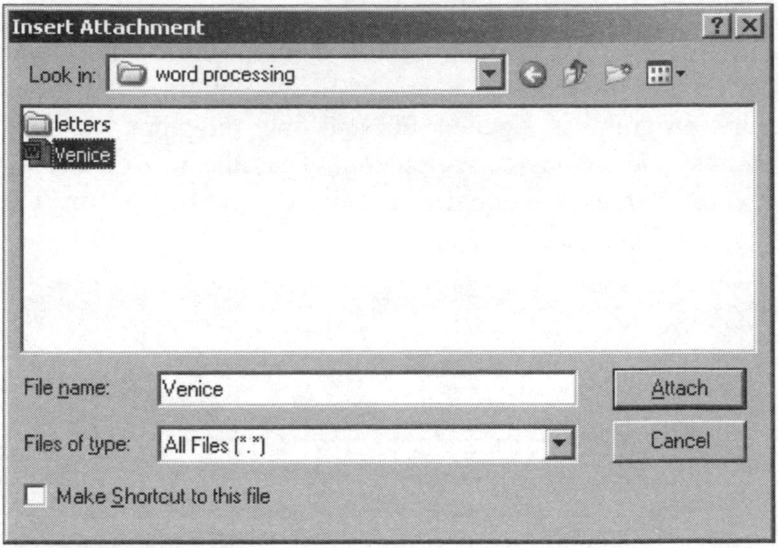

In the above **Insert Attachment** dialogue box, open up the drop-down menu on the right of the **Look in** bar. Then select the folder containing the Word file which is to be sent as an e-mail attachment. I have opened a folder called **word processing** and selected the file called **Venice**. Now click **Attach** and the name of the selected file will appear on the top of the e-mail message as shown below, to the right of **Attach**.

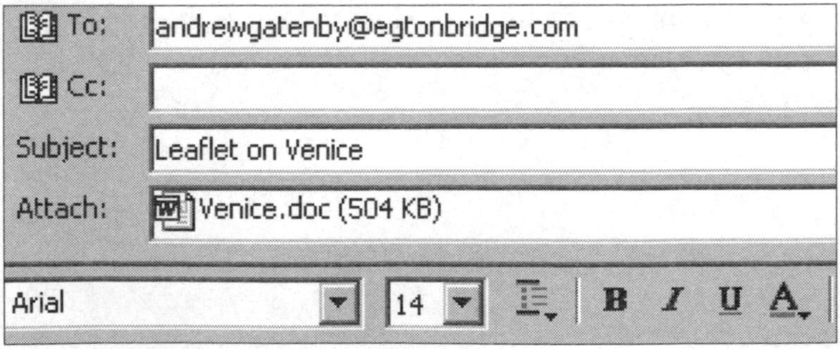

The e-mail and its attachment are now ready to send as a single entity. When the recipient looks at their e-mail **Inbox**, the e-mail message is listed along with a paper-clip icon denoting the presence of an attachment.

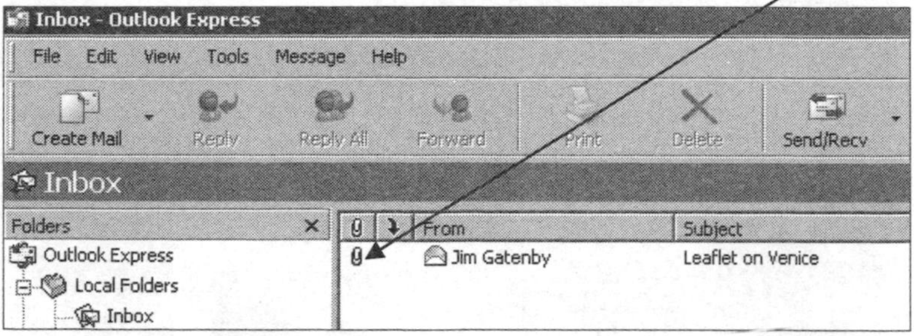

When the recipient double clicks the e-mail to open it, the file name and icon for the attachment appear next to the word **Attach** as shown above. If you now double-click the attachment name or icon, the following dialogue box appears, giving you the chance to open the document, in this case a Word document.

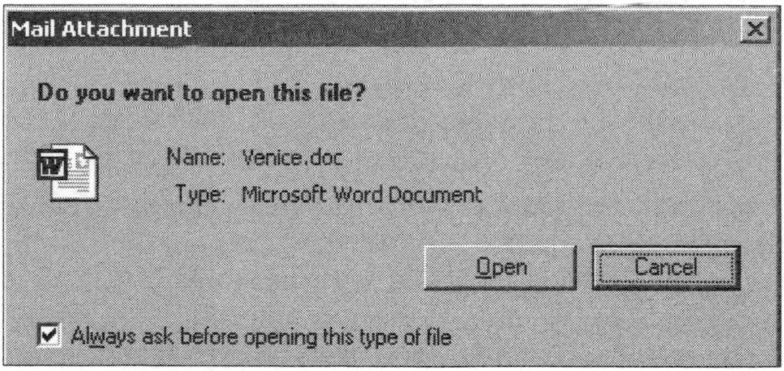

If the recipient feels confident that the e-mail and its attachment are from a genuine source, then they click **Open** as shown on the previous page. In this example, the Word program opens displaying the Venice leaflet which has been sent as an e-mail attachment.

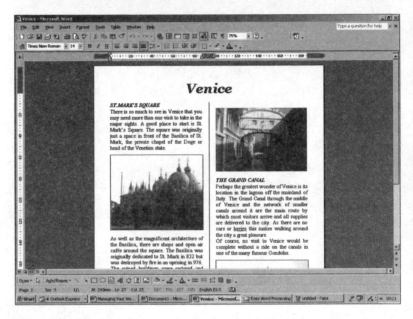

The recipient of the e-mail can now read the Word document. If necessary they could make changes to the text then e-mail the amended version back to the sender for further discussion.

I have used these methods to send whole chapters of books to the printers, saving several days compared with the conventional letter post. For very large files, such as a complete book, you really need to be using a *broadband* Internet system – otherwise the times for uploading (sending) and downloading (receiving) are too great.

Viruses in Word Files

The **Mail Attachment** dialogue box which appears when you attempt to open an attachment contains a warning about the dangers of opening files received from the Internet.

Viruses are small programs, usually written by malicious young men, and designed to cause damage and inconvenience to computer users. A virus may simply display a "humorous" message or it may cause the entire contents of a hard disc to be destroyed. There are thousands of different viruses and a huge industry producing anti-virus software designed to intercept and destroy them.

Word files can themselves contain viruses and files sent as e-mail attachments have the potential to spread viruses between computers. So if you are unfortunate enough to pick up a virus on your machine, you might also contaminate the computers of your friends or colleagues. The source of a virus on your machine might be a floppy disc, CD or e-mail of dubious origin.

Anti-Virus Software

It's essential that your computer is equipped with up-to-date anti-virus software. Well-known brands include Norton AntiVirus, McAfee VirusScan and F-Secure. Typical prices are in the range £20-£40; this could save a great deal of time and inconvenience if a damaging infection is prevented. The software should also include regular updates to the *virus definitions*. These should enable the anti-virus software to detect and destroy the very latest viruses, which are constantly being invented.

The F-Secure Internet Security package illustrated below also includes Internet Protection as well as virus protection. The Internet Shield is designed to prevent "hackers" gaining unauthorized access to your computer over the Internet.

Appendix 1
Cutting, Copying and Pasting

Earlier in this book the use of the clipboard as a temporary storage area was discussed. The clipboard can be used for the following tasks:

- Moving text and graphics from one part of a Word document to another.

- Moving and copying text and graphics between different programs such as copying an image from a painting program into Word. Extracts from other applications such as spreadsheet and database programs can also be copied into Word.

- As discussed in the last chapter, the clipboard can also be used in the Windows Explorer when moving or copying files and folders to different locations, such as a different folder or a different disc.

The basic method is that text and/or graphics (or files and folders) are selected so that they appear highlighted on the screen. (In a drawing program such as Microsoft Paint, an area of a picture is selected using the rectangular selection tool.) The selected text or graphics is then copied to the clipboard using **Edit** and **Copy** from the Menu Bar. If you want to *move* the selected text and/or graphics then use **Edit** and **Cut** from the Menu Bar. **Cut** removes the selected material from its original location. In Word, in addition to the **Edit** menu there are also **Cut, Copy** and **Paste** icons on the Toolbar.

The **Cut** and **Copy** operations are the main methods of placing objects such as text, graphics, files and folders on the clipboard. However, a copy of the current screen display can also be placed on the clipboard using the **Print Scrn** key, as discussed earlier. Once on the clipboard, items are placed in new locations using the **Paste** command off the **Edit** menu. For example, after placing an image from a drawing program on the clipboard, you might open up Word and paste the image onto the Word page at the current cursor position.

It's possible to do all of your cutting, copying and pasting on single objects, one at a time. However, Microsoft Office XP, of which Word is a part, provides the Office Clipboard, in addition to the basic system Clipboard. The Office Clipboard can be used to temporarily store multiple items and paste them into various locations. To view the Office Clipboard in Word select **Edit** and **Office Clipboard**....The clipboard appears in its own pane on the right of the Word screen. The Office Clipboard can store up to 24 cut or

copied items. The example on the right has two items, an extract from a graphics program and a piece of text from Word. Each item has an individual drop-down menu with **Paste** and **Delete** options. Buttons at the top allow you to **Paste All** or **Clear All** items. An **Options** menu at the bottom of the pane allows you to select the way the Office Clipboard is displayed.

Appendix 2
Using the Mail Merge Feature in Word

This facility is a time-saver for anyone who needs to send the same basic letter to lots of different people. The mail merge is particularly useful for club secretaries, etc., and organizations with a large mailing list. The basic letter only has to be typed once; this is then used as a template to produce a large number of personalized letters. The main features of the mail merge are:

- The basic letter, most of which is the same for everyone
- "Place holders" in the standard letter into which personal details such as name and address are filled
- A data source or file which is a list of all of the names and addresses, etc., of the people who are to receive the letter
- The merge process itself which infills the details of each person, enabling individual personalized letters to be printed.

The **Mail Merge Wizard** is very easy to use and guides you through the process giving instructions at each stage. (Word also has a Mail Merge Toolbar which can be displayed by clicking **View**, **Toolbars** and **Mail Merge**.)

To start the **Mail Merge Wizard**, in the Word program select **Tools**, **Letters and Mailings** and **Mail Merge Wizard....** The Mail Merge Wizard opens in a pane on the right-hand side of the Word screen, as shown on the next page.

First you select **Letters** from a list of document types, by clicking on the appropriate radio button. Then you click **Next** at the bottom of the Mail Merge pane to move onto **Step 2** of the wizard. Here you select **Use the current document** and start typing in the basic letter in the main Word window. (You can edit the basic text of the letter later if you wish).

Next you need to create a list of recipients or select an existing list. We need to create a new list so click **Type a new list**. Click the **Create** button shown on the right. Then you have to enter the names and addresses, etc., of all of the people who are to receive the letter, as shown on the next page.

Once created as a file on disc this list of names and addresses can be called up and used whenever you want to send a "mail shot" to all of your contacts, etc.

New Address List

Enter Address information

Address Line 1	14, Vernon St
Address Line 2	Radbourne
City	Oxford
State	Oxfordshire
ZIP Code	OX54 6RA
Country	England
Home Phone	
Work Phone	

| New Entry | Delete Entry | Find Entry ... | Filter and Sort... | Customize... |

View Entries

View Entry Number   First | Previous | 1 | Next | Last

Total entries in list   2

Close

When you have entered all of the details of the recipients of the letter, click **Close** and you are asked to save the addresses, etc., as a database file with a name of your choice, as shown in the following fictitious extract.

Mail Merge Recipients

To sort the list, click the appropriate column heading. To narrow down the recipients displayed by a specific criteria, such as by city, click the arrow next to the column heading. Use the check boxes or buttons to add or remove recipients from the mail merge.

List of recipients:

	Last Name	First Name	Title	Company Name	Address Line
☑	Gatenby	Andrew	Mr.	Andrew Gatenby Ltd	Goatland Farm
☑	Austin	Jill	Miss	Martins Bank	Market Place

The wizard now tells you to write your letter in the main pane in the centre of the screen, if you have not already done so. At this stage you also enter the place holders for the personal information to be added to each letter.

225

For example, place the cursor at the point in the letter where you want the recipient's address to start and click **Address block...** off the Mail Merge wizard, as shown on the right. You are given a choice of formats for the address block and having chosen one, click **OK**. The place holder **<<Address Block>>** is placed in the document at the current cursor position as shown below. This is repeated for other information such as the **Greeting line...** (as in Dear Jill, etc.)

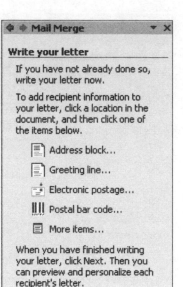

Write your letter

If you have not already done so, write your letter now.

To add recipient information to your letter, click a location in the document, and then click one of the items below.

- Address block...
- Greeting line...
- Electronic postage...
- Postal bar code...
- More items...

When you have finished writing your letter, click Next. Then you can preview and personalize each recipient's letter.

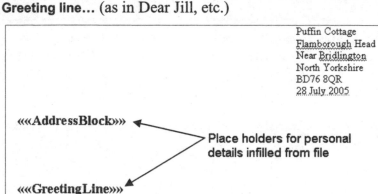

```
                                            Puffin Cottage
                                            Flamborough Head
                                            Near Bridlington
                                            North Yorkshire
                                            BD76 8QR
                                            28 July 2005

   ««AddressBlock»»  ◄─────────┐
                                 ╲──►  Place holders for personal
                                 ╱       details infilled from file
   ««GreetingLine»»  ◄─────────┘

   I am writing to all members of the club to let you know that our next trip will be
```

Next the Mail Merge wizard allows you to preview the finished letters with the personal information added. There are buttons to scroll through each of the individual letters.

Finally click **Next** to complete the merge and print the letters.

Index